Diderot,
inside, outside, & in-between

Coda Press, Inc., 700 West Badger Road, Suite 101, Madison, WI 53713
Library of Congress Cataloging in Publication Data

Undank, Jack.
    Diderot—inside, outside, and in-between.

    Includes bibliographical references.
    1. Diderot, Denis, 1713–1784—Criticism and interpretation. I. Title.
PQ1979.Ud   848'.5'09   79-14210
ISBN 0-930956-08-7
ISBN 0-930956-09-5 pbk.
Also available from Coda Press, Inc.

Jack Undank

DIDEROT

Inside,
Outside,
&
In-Between

Coda Press, Inc., 700 West Badger Road, Suite 101,
Madison, Wisconsin 53713

preface

This essay, like all others, emerges from a question or desire that it obscures rather than resolves. I wanted to understand my admiration for Diderot's literary personality; I was not at all sure where that personality could be located. What do we mean by Diderot's "thought" or "achievement," if not a public and historical scraping of his language? I had in mind qualities more deeply active in that language, and I might have stopped at its texture or style, at what my colleague, Milton Seiden, calls its "tone" and "presence." (Outside of Spitzer's article, I can think of no examination of Diderot's style that produces the yield of Croll's more syntactic studies of stylistic "periods.") In any case, I decided to discover, if I could, the impulse that governs even style or, more broadly, rhetoric, in the phenomenological transactions of a literary subjectivity and its world, the making of an individual speech with and within the coordinates (reader, subject matter, "given" discourse) of any utterance. Such a speech positions itself and receives its specificity or "personality" with respect to those coordinates—at least that has been my working hypothesis. If I am right, then in this perspective, position is indeed everything in the author's life. I've tried to make it clear—but without implacably dotting every "i" in this matter or any other—that this position, as much a strain as a natural flexing of temperament and desire, maintains its stability or process not without misgivings and always against or inside the plasticities of a social and cultural milieu. Since the space of eighteenth-century literary consciousness is not fully charted, I preferred to hint at possible paths rather than to fix any one with permanent marking stones.

My spatial metaphors betray my debts, first and foremost to Diderot, who lived through them and so provided his own clues, but also to a host of aestheticians and theorists of literary space whose names will spring to mind in these pages without first being mentioned here. If this essay can be said to have a thesis, it would be, I think, that as sentimentality intensifies, so too does its dialectical complement, irony, whose nature through the eighteenth century suffers an enduring change. I could not have arrived at this conclusion without the insight of Alan Wilde, who first indicated to me the bizarre but necessary coupling of these terms and who coined the expression "anironic" in an effort to frame the same enduring and complex polarities in modern and postmodern literature. I hope he will accept this essay as only part of an infinitely vaster debt.

My thanks, finally, go to the Research Council of Rutgers University, for its encouragement and sponsorship, and to Carl Lovitt of Coda Press, for his sympathetic and dynamic support.

contents

Catherine's thigh

Even if the story about Diderot's thumping the thighs
of Catherine the Great were apocryphal,[1] it would come in
handy as a blueprint for a kind of intense negotiation in
which the energies of intelligence act out their physical and
spatial implications. We might say that the perlocutionary
force of what Diderot was saying spells itself out in
Catherine's bruises. The bruises don't, as they might in
Sade, demonstrate the point of an argument by making it
visible. Diderot's argument is irrelevant here. It isn't, in any
case, the message that leaves the mark, but a hand crossing
space, surreptitiously encoding a desire to overcome
distance, to ratify an understanding, to appropriate an
alien consciousness by some supplementary physical act.
The hand doesn't merely accompany the overt verbal
message. We have to imagine it as only the visible
outcropping of a movement passing through the message
—a sign of what the message intends and also, perhaps, of
its inspiration. The message and the bruise are delivered

[1]Arthur M. Wilson, *Diderot* (New York: Oxford University Press,
1970), pp. 632–33.

together—a double assault, not meant to disseminate merely, but to capture and convert. It is as if there were no true knowledge without intimacy, the interposition of a personhood, to confirm it; or as if complicity in fact were the end of knowledge. Diderot, with his burden of encyclopedic wisdom, can't rely solely on facts and opinions or the persuasions of language but has to remind the Empress that he is the medium. His hand falls on her thigh like the reinforcement of a narrative frame, the subtle, barely conscious index of an outsidedness which is, paradoxically, the guarantee of what Michael Polanyi would call "personal knowledge." His hand closes a distance but certifies his presence.

The story would be of little importance if we were not inclined to think of it as characteristic. In spatializing some of the dimensions of the dilemma of what we've come to call—abstractly, generically, as though it could be considered without its phenomenological implications—vulgarization, the story points toward a specifically personal transaction. Personal, but, as I hope to conclude, not entirely eccentric. It tells us that, in the process of Diderot's presentations, the self extrudes seductively and irresistibly beyond the limits of its discourse. To acknowledge that this is a hazard, a risk occasioned by temperament and design, leading to an awkward self-awareness, we need only remember that Catherine decided to put a table between herself and the philosopher. But the table is precisely the boundary of discourse. Thrown back within his words, within the substance of what he anxiously transmits, Diderot's hands, now invisibly rhetorical, continue to flutter—even to grow conscious of themselves. This is of course what interests us, the gesture *within* language, here a supposition (Catherine's interest extends only to palpable effects), but everywhere evident in Diderot's work and, indeed, in Diderot's spectacular concern with the gestural and spatial basis of language itself.

Still, the *tableau vivant* of the Empress and the philosopher tells us more, especially if we set the scene in the context of a larger action. Diderot, traveling to Russia not as a salesman for his Encyclopedia but as its embodiment, is there to be tapped. If Pierre Janet was right in believing that the origins of intelligence go back to a notion of transportation, the mind taking over the function of the simple carrying basket ("la conduite du panier"), Diderot nicely figures the porter and the basket itself, overcoming, in this wider focus, the distances of geography and time.[2] He is replete with knowledge, joined to it; it is inside him or he moves within it. This is to suggest that two proximate, vehicular desires converge in the scene of Catherine and Diderot: one, already fulfilled, that draws Diderot toward close intimacy with a body of knowledge; the other, being enacted, that seeks to capture another "body," the listener's or reader's—both, impulses to assimilate and appropriate. Catherine's innocent rejection, Diderot's path from spontaneity to awareness or, we might say, his fall from invisibility to presence, reveals the illusory nature of the project, as

[2]See François Dagognet, *Ecriture et iconographie* (Paris: J. Vrin, 1973), p. 10, and also the concluding chapter: "Unité et actualité de Diderot, Théoricien du Télé-visuel."

doomed and irrepressible as Narcissus closing the gap between himself and his image. There is no beginning and no end to this incident, first because it comes to us as a biographical fragment, and then, more importantly, because it's here being purveyed as a paradigm of the intentional form of Diderot's work. His project, always "winning near the goal," and therefore condemned to repeat itself, before and after Catherine, pushes and continues to push on greedily toward further objects and bodies, even toward an imagined posterity, a temporal transfer making amends for the deficiencies of a spatial "conduite du panier."

> quoique cette matière soit assez
> difficile et s'étende un peu au-delà
> de vos connaissances mathématiques,
> je ne désespérerais pas, en me
> préparant, de la mettre à votre
> portée, et de vous initier dans cette
> logique infinitésimale.
>
> *Lettre sur les aveugles*

Diderot begins and ends his career as a vulgarizer. The epigraph, with its polite condescension and control, makes him sound for a moment like Fontenelle. Between *je* and *vous* there is the hope of a conventionally pedagogical relationship: subject matter, preparation, initiation set in logical sequence. What is distinctive about Diderot and seals the difference between him and his predecessors will upset this tone and the neat boundaries of this sequence. The epigraph serves therefore as the marker for a starting point, not as a summary of the race. I do not mean, either, to install Diderot schematically between the Newtonian *Lettre sur la résistance de l'air* and the Senecan *Essai sur les règnes de Claude et de Néron,* but to suggest that all of Diderot's presentations or imitations (genres as diverse as an article for the Encyclopedia, a translation, a work of fiction) are re-presentations, re-enactments of things grasped and experienced, often second-hand. People like Paul Vernière and myself have vexed the last participle, the now dim or tired life-into-art formulation, but I'm here casting my net more widely to include the experience of texts and artworks and to emphasize the peculiar urgency not just of reworking but of relaying things and words from one place to another, one condition to another, one person to another. If there are works by Diderot that seem at first glance far afield from vulgarization, *La Religieuse, Le Neveu de Rameau, Le Fils naturel,* for example, it is only because the vulgarizing procedures—Diderot as intermediary between object and audience—are, on occasion, structurally internalized and transferred to fictional voices, and even more strikingly, because the *problem* of re-presentation becomes thematized. More of these complexities later on. At some necessarily conjectural beginning, there is simply the object (subject matter, text) and Diderot's enthrallment with it, the special tension between the writer and his borrowed discourse, an anxiety of trust (G. Steiner's term) and abandon, and also the simultaneous awareness of a third party, the reader, to whom Diderot addresses himself. In this inaugural context, no work could be more exemplary than Diderot's translation of Shaftesbury's *Inquiry concerning Virtue, or Merit:* a repetition designed for transfer (*transferre > translatus*), a species of "imitation" as Dryden understood it, and also a patent act of vulgarization.[3]

As it happens—and I think it is not coincidental—Shaftesbury's essay concerns itself with an ethic of what

[3] Blake Hanna, in an unpublished dissertation, "Les débuts intellectuels de Denis Diderot" (Montréal, 1964), is right on target, I believe, when he says: "La traduction n'a jamais été qu'une étape pour le futur Philosophe et Encyclopédiste. Sa véritable vocation est celle d'un vulgarisateur, dans le meilleur sens du terme. Rien ne témoigne de cette vocation d'une façon plus éloquente que sa réaction devant la traduction de Shaftesbury" (p. 339).

might be called imitative harmony, emanations and exchanges of sympathy. Riding on the counterflow to Hobbesian and other, French, especially Jansenist, varieties of theories of egocentricity, Shaftesbury's "social affection" sets down, as we know, a philosophic base for social unity. After the solipsisms of Descartes and Berkeley, the need for divine grace or divine mediation between consciousness and any outside object, Shaftesbury proposes the cognitive immediacy of human feeling and intelligence dialectically deployed: each man with the instinct of an artist, imitating nature, reproducing in his actions the beautifully cohesive forces of an immanent God. "Avoir les affections sociales entières . . . c'est suivre pas à pas la nature; c'est imiter, c'est représenter l'Etre suprême, sous une forme humaine."[4] To avoid modern confusions, we ought to note that imitation, as this quotation implies, slips knowingly back to its medieval past, to its personally redemptive and social, as opposed to its more strictly aesthetic, role. But Augustinian

[4]I take advantage of the new *Oeuvres complètes* (Paris: Hermann, 1970–) now in progress, to draw quotations from those volumes that have appeared. This quotation comes from Vol. I, p. 387. Henceforth, references to collections of Diderot's works will appear in the text. Those drawn from Assézat-Tourneux (Paris: Garnier, 1875–77) will be referred to as "A-T," from Hermann as "H," from Vernière's *Oeuvres philosophiques* (Paris: Garnier, 1956) as "V, *O.p.*," his *Oeuvres esthétiques* (Garnier, 1959) as "V, *O.e.*," Bénac's *Oeuvres romanesques* (Garnier, 1959) as "B, *O.r.*," G. Roth's and J. Varloot's *Correspondance* (Paris: Minuit, 1955–70) as "Roth." Titles of articles from the *Encyclopédie* will appear in upper case letters. References to works by other authors will be given, after their first citation, parenthetically in the text. The English translations in the Appendix are my own.

caritas, with its triangular path of Reason through the life and body of Christ, from creature to creature, is insidiously transformed. Christ vanishes; God suffuses man and the world with a moral-aesthetic electricity; human connection travels more directly. When Shaftesbury invokes reflection (the "reflected sense"), it is only to recharge or redirect some depleted or vagrant battery. A life of virtue or merit may be an effortless or at least a habitual imitation. It may also be an "enthusiastic" one. What it proposes as its joyous fulfilment is a fusion of the self with nature and with other selves, a merger so empathetically complete that the old antinomies of reason and passion, mind and body, nature and art, give up their categorical ghosts. Remnants of the Augustinian model subsist. Fundamentally man is not thought but desire, there is still a primal quest for happiness,[5] and it still involves a union with God. But God is now dispersed through the world and his creatures, and happiness, accessible *in saeculo.*

It turns out—and this is why I appear to digress—that the subject matter of Shaftesbury's *Inquiry* coordinates startlingly with the procedures of Diderot's translation. It is as if, with the translations of Stanyon and James behind him, Diderot falls on the philosophical justification for his

[5]It is not at all noticed that some of Diderot's speculations on happiness are profoundly Augustinian, possibly as a result of Shaftesbury but more likely of his religious training. The happy "méchant" will always be, for Diderot, either a physiological mutant, a "bad seed," or someone who has drunk deep of Augustine's "inebriate wine of the inverted will," a man reaching for the good, but misdirected. The Good draws desire like a magnet.

activity. And the activity, which forms a bond between French readers and an English author, erecting bridges and equivalencies, constitutes as well, especially as Diderot handles the job, an act of personal sympathy, a technical instance of Shaftesbury's more general philosophy. What is, on the surface of it, a social philosophy meets with a linguistic response that catches its reflection and recapitulates its motions. At this juncture, however covertly, something vastly important is taking place in the manner of *vulgarisation*. It has little to do with whether Diderot favored the school of "free" translation (Desfontaines, Prévost) over the school of the "literal" (Coste, Silhouette) —a point that teases so many of Diderot's editors—since in this light Diderot comes off not too tellingly as an interloper in two camps. More fundamentally, the issue is the space he prefers to occupy as he translates and transmits, his relationship to the text before him, his *Einfühlung*, the intensity of his response, and his awareness of the reader. Which is to say that, more fully than his vulgarizing predecessors, Diderot is swept, willingly and willfully, into a hermeneutic motion that compels him to close or challenge every gap that separates him from his model.

Later on, in his *De l'Interprétation de la nature,* after exclaiming, "Hâtons-nous de rendre la philosophie populaire," Diderot will speak of "la bonne méthode et la longue habitude" (A-T, II, 38–39) that ought to make the effort practicable. But the habit is being formed and the method already visible in the Shaftesbury translation. If Shaftesbury's notion of imitation, as we've seen, invites us to search out the harmonious message beneath nature's display and to see its repetition in human acts or works of art, Diderot's rechristening of the *Inquiry* as *Principes de la philosophie morale* tells us that Shaftesbury's thought, as Diderot sees it, has its peculiar unity that merely ramifies organically what its root network (ethos) absorbs and establishes. Shaftesbury encourages this view. His notes consist of cross-references to his other works. And to judge from Diderot's reworking of several textual passages and from his own footnotes which, in part, spell out the content of Shaftesbury's cross-references, Diderot had steeped himself in the entire Shaftesburyan brew. Yet, as if this weren't enough, the exercise is served up with two introductories—a letter to his pious brother ("A mon frère") and a "Discours préliminaire" in which Diderot makes clear what he discovered to be Shaftesbury's principles: to treat virtue apart from religious dogma ("Il n'est question dans cet Essai que de la vertu morale . . ." [H, I, 296]) and to make of it a social, binding impulse as natural as the instinctive appreciation of natural and artistic beauty. The principles are also the message when it is honed to a cutting edge. Diderot here, as throughout the translation, aims at what he takes to be essential, providing us with a French shorthand for Shaftesbury, but a shorthand controlled by an interpretive energy, a "preunderstanding" he doesn't fully acknowledge. Critics have noticed how much shorter the translation is than the original, and they have ascribed this to the mythical incisiveness of French. But this is to overlook the fact that Shaftesbury's syntax and vocabulary radiate moods and emphases that Diderot's pointed and independent elegance cannot "translate" but rather deflates to an urgency that is foreign to the original.[6] Ideologically and linguistically, Diderot cuts through Shaftesbury's lyric caution and compound prose to what he reads beneath as a generative center, Shaftesbury's "spirit": "Je l'ai lu et relu; je me suis rempli de son esprit, et j'ai, pour ainsi dire, fermé son livre, lorsque j'ai pris la plume" (H, I, 300). Diderot's extraordinary receptivity, like the welcoming of a long-dreamed-of Entelechy, quickens into possessiveness and

---

[6]This happens so regularly that only one example, at random, may illustrate what I mean. SHAFTESBURY: "But to proceed from what is esteemed mere goodness, and lies within the reach and capacity of all sensible creatures, to that which is called virtue or merit, and is allowed to man only" (*Characteristics*, ed. John M. Robertson [London: Grant Richards, 1900], I, 251). DIDEROT: "Mais pour passer de cette bonté pure et simple dont toute créature sensible est capable, à cette qualité qu'on appelle *vertu* et qui convient ici-bas à l'homme seul" (H, I, 320). Diderot omits the subtle irony behind the participle "esteemed"; he drops "merit" as a qualifying appositive to "virtue"; he neutralizes the slightly theological ring of "allowed" by using "convient" in its place, and he adds "ici-bas" as if to insist on the wholly naturalistic character of virtue.

finally command.[7] When his pleasure and assent are greatest, and, to use the words of his editors, "il lui arrive d'abonder dans le sens de son partenaire, de renchérir sur ses affirmations" (H, I, 280), he directs and manipulates his "partner," compressing, prolonging, or stressing Shaftesbury's meanings and movements.[8] The process seems sexual or alimentary, Diderot, the "*latus*," bringing matter to life, releasing its inherent energies, as he will in *Le Rêve de d'Alembert,* by ingesting it (V, *O.p.,* 263). He in fact so completely assimilates Shaftesbury that years later he will blamefully attribute to him, in the article BEAU, a certain notion of beauty as organic functionalism, a notion he himself had contrived in a footnote to the *Inquiry* (H, I, 324), memory putting asunder what the spell of translation once joined and engendered.

If we can locate originality or independence in Diderot's text, it may be said to reverberate from his source —a concept for which the source, as I have said, itself

[7] According to George Steiner in *After Babel: Aspects of Language and Translation* (New York and London: Oxford University Press, 1975), p. 26: "There is a strain of femininity in the great interpreter, a submission, made active by intensity of response, to the creative presence." Steiner is bound to raise feminist hackles. To readjust the scales and to make the male-female polarity fade into androgyny, I must record Barbey d'Aurevilly's impression of Diderot: "C'est un épouseur de sujets. Il entre en eux et les féconde." See *Goethe et Diderot* (Paris: Dentu, 1880), p. 219 (cited by Georges May, in his edition of François Hemsterhuis' *Lettre sur l'homme* [New Haven: Yale University Press, 1964], p. 15).

[8] In the "Discours préliminaire," Diderot acknowledges that "on n'a jamais usé du bien d'autrui avec tant de liberté" (H, I, 300).

provides an ideological ground. In a note elaborating on Shaftesbury's comparison of people's affections and the strings of a musical instrument, Diderot first draws attention to the idea of interpersonal vibrations and concludes: "Cette comparaison pourrait être poussée bien loin, car le son excité est toujours analogue à celui qui l'excite" (H, I, 374). Between instruments there remains always some subtle monophony: a sound transposed, for example, from violin to harpsichord continues to bear the imprint of the violin. It is impossible to detect the faintest trill of Oedipal anxiety in Diderot's harpsichord, which settles very appropriately into the landscape of Shaftesbury's vision of imitative harmonies. Every "originality" comes as a rendition of and a projection back to a source, a repetition whose instrumental register partly displaces and replaces a heard melody. So it would seem, until—carrying the analogy still further—we realize that the "excited sound" disperses and travels not only toward its source, but all around; becomes, in other words, a source itself. There is some tricky evidence that Diderot may have understood this in a passage from Shaftesbury he distorts, or at any rate, complicates. The reflective mind, mulling over "characters or pictures of manners," says Shaftesbury, "readily discerns the good and ill toward the species or public"[9]—a rather passive discrimination. Yet Diderot translates the last phrase as "saisit avec promptitude et *rend avec vivacité* et le bien et le mal" (H, I, 325; my italics). This rendering of Shaftesbury, which insists on the *rend*ering, the "vivacious return" or

[9]*Characteristics*, I, 252.

depiction of received impressions, a repayment in kind, threatens to predicate, as the sentence would have it, an exchange of evil for evil as well as good for good (unthinkable in Shaftesbury himself). Unless, that is, Diderot meant, by translating "discerns" into "saisit" and "rendre," to stress the independently active qualities of even the mind in recollection, its urge both to grasp *and* to broadcast. In any case, Diderot's "originalities" do in fact appear in the way he nudges and promotes Shaftesbury as if from within Shaftesbury's discourse, in the way he manages, while absorbing and absorbed, to gesture to his readers, to emerge rhetorically from under Shaftesbury's cover. Typically, in the passage I've just mentioned, where Diderot's alterations are otherwise in low relief, we come upon these lines whose rhetoric commentators have ignored:

Shaftesbury	Diderot
In these vagrant characters or pictures of manners, which the mind of necessity figures to itself and carries still about with it, the heart cannot possibly remain neutral; but constantly takes part one way or another. However false or corrupt it be within itself, it finds the difference, as to beauty and comeliness, between one heart and another . . .	Mais le coeur regarde-t-il avec indifférence les esquisses des moeurs que l'esprit est forcé de tracer, et qui lui sont presque toujours présentes? *Je* m'en rapporte au sentiment intérieur. Il *me* dit qu'aussi nécessité dans ses jugements, que l'esprit dans ses opéra-tions, sa corruption ne va jamais jusqu'à lui dérober totalement la différence du beau et du laid . . . (my italics)

Diderot tests Shaftesbury's hypothesis on some trans-personal and exemplary "I," a self that prolongs Shaftesbury's but contrives, in part, to be Diderot's own, and also a magnet for the reader's. Diderot responds, we might say, like Shaftesbury's "heart," which "cannot possibly remain neutral; but constantly takes part one way or another." And as he does, he prepares for his entry by shaping a declarative into a curtain-raising question. Here, as in Diderot's own footnotes, when a first-person appears, the voice is an equivocal projection. "Divin anachorète," one such footnote begins, "suspendez un moment la profondeur de vos méditations" (H, I, 311). It is an apostrophe that addresses and, in the process, concretizes Shaftesbury's vague textual image of the solitary man. As Jonathan Culler has explained,[10] any apostrophe calls forth a unique

[10]Paper delivered at the Charles Sanders Peirce Symposium on Semiotics and the Arts, The Johns Hopkins University, September 25-26, 1975. Diderot's tendency to apostrophize appears to have grown much stronger with age, his apostrophes to have amplified into oracular injunctions—in the *Supplément au voyage de Bougainville,* the *Observations* for Catherine, the *Essai sur les règnes de Claude et de Néron,* and in the "écriture fragmentaire" of Raynal's *Histoire des deux Indes.* See on this point, the richly suggestive work by Michèle Duchet, *Diderot et l'Histoire des Deux Indes, ou l'Ecriture Fragmentaire* (Paris: Nizet, 1978), p. 11, n. 10 and pp. 172–74. Apostrophes allow Diderot to be both fixed within his subject matter and to levitate morally, tonally, and fearlessly above it, under the cloak of a fictive or uncontrollably inspired voice: "Elevé au-dessus de toutes les considérations humaines, c'est alors qu'on plane au-dessus de l'atmosphère . . . C'est là que j'ai pu véritablement m'écrier, je suis libre, et me sentir au niveau de mon sujet" (cited in Duchet, p. 164).

triadic transaction between subject, object, and audience, its specific function, to draw attention to a passionate speaker's exemplary behavior. And so Diderot speaks here, and as the passage continues, as a supplement to Shaftesbury, a voice that becomes a new but monstrous textual substance. Can we tell where its sound is carrying? If the apostrophe speaks to the "anachorète," and we over-hear it, in another footnote, Diderot's first, the voice turns directly to the reader: "Remarquez," it exhorts, "qu'il est question de la religion en général" (H, I, 302). Diderot stalks the text, as usual, but the sentence actually hovers between his text, himself, and us. It points to or enjoins all three, as Diderot pivots to align himself with Shaftesbury, to order his understanding, and finally ours.[11] The series

---

This "niveau de mon sujet" can be described as the subject matter's furthest eventuality, its political efflorescence—a level at which the matter may be spoken *of* and acted upon. Rooted in exposition, another discourse, hortatory, conclusive, rises away from it (toward a *narrataire*). This apostrophizing and emerging movement parallels, I believe, what Duchet brilliantly perceives as Diderot's contribution to Raynal's *Histoire,* and her thesis could easily be extended to Diderot's less fragmentary writings and to his rhetoric in general: "De fragment en fragment, Diderot en est venu à ce discours *sur* l'histoire qui trouve son unité dans le même lieu où il s'installe" (p. 175).

[11] In his review of the Club français du livre edition of Diderot's works (*Critique*, 296 [1972]), Jean Starobinski quotes from Grimm's report, in the *Correspondance littéraire* of 1782, on Diderot's *Essai sur les règnes de Claude et de Néron,* a passage remarkable for its focus on the way, at the other end of his literary life, Diderot makes his personae apostrophize to the point of confusing identities: "Il faut prendre son parti de voir l'auteur . . . s'adresser tantôt aux maîtres du monde, tantôt

of questions, the "vous" that follows repeatedly—usually offered as examples of Diderot's early temptation to dialogue—only reinforce the impression that Diderot, once inside Shaftesbury's text and its principles, is expelled by the vibrations it produces in him and by the need to set off a comparable "enjoyment of good" in others. First, in Shaftesbury's words, "a receiving of it, as it were, by

---

aux derniers roquets de la littérature, et, dans son enthousiasme dramatique . . . s'apostropher lui-même, apostropher ses lecteurs et leur laisser souvent l'embarras de chercher quel est le personnage qu'il fait parler, ou quel est celui auquel il s'adresse" (p. 9). There could be no better testimony to the fact that Diderot's pivoting movement, like his other rhetorical gestures, comes to inhabit, implosively, the internal and interpersonal world of his narratives.

Starobinski uses this citation to support his demonstration of how Diderot creates, as translator and reiterator, a defensive cover for his own speech, an authoritative "objectification" in "la parole des autres" of his vulnerable and threatened presence or message. Slightly modifying but also complementing this interpretation, my own reading stresses the technical processes of Diderot's works, the ironic and self-conscious tensions in his "transfers" and in his involvements with readers. As a result, where Starobinski sees an "aliénation consentie" (p. 13) that eventuates at the end of Diderot's life in a "pure indépendence" (p. 20), a fearless voice speaking "la vérité entière" (p. 21) for the first time and only in view of the final objectification bestowed by death, I find a single though repeated *phase* of self-forgetful assent, always accompanied or followed by a recuperative wakefulness. Though Starobinski would shun an Oedipal interpretation, his developmental stress as well as his insistence on a tactical and political sublimation, Diderot's progress from "docility" and "depersonalization" to "aggression," from imitative "mask" to bold independence and a voice (virility) of his own, make a fair case for one.

reflection, or by way of participation,"[12] followed by the desire, in Diderot's interpolated and emphatic phrase, "de communiquer aux autres les plaisirs qu'on ressent" (H, I, 384).

---

[12] *Characteristics*, I, 298.

transcription and witness

As the universal interlocutor (*allocutaire*), God still hovers in the wings of Diderot's notes to the *Inquiry*. Paraphrasing Shaftesbury's "Hymn to Nature" (from *The Moralists*), a commonplace of baroque religious literature, in which a dramatized persona loses himself in the ecstatic contemplation of an infinite universe, Diderot symptomaically introduces a parallel text from Cicero's *Academica*. The ecstasy turns out to be redundant, part of an ancient "écho des siècles" (Diderot's expression for it, elsewhere[13]), a perennial, human testimony, here linked in intertextual transcription. And then, at the end of the paraphrase, Diderot invents a special "satisfaction" for his contemplator: the pleasure of finding himself "sous les yeux de la divinité" (H, I, 359). The viewer is home safe because he is, happily, viewed; lost ("cette contemplation qui l'anéantit . . ."), but now found, his presence restored and confirmed by divine witness—or, paradoxically, by the eyes of the narrator. This divinity, absent from the rest of Diderot's account, does not so much subtend the immensity of nature ("l'immensité des êtres"), the *speculum mundi,* as it subscribes to a human thereness. If a mirror, then one that returns man's image, comforting him with the sight of himself. The contemplator, first lodged in an unbroken chain of human witnesses, then witnessed, self-witnesed, witnessed from on high or from the plane of a narrative projection—all of this is premonitory.

[13]*Pensées détachées sur la peinture*, V, *O.e.*, 756.

Eventually, even this pale mirror of a divinity will disappear from Diderot's sight, leaving the universe as a given "work" (vital, self-generating, and, like the Scriptures in Spinoza's *Tractatus*, divorced from symbol and support), and only the human view, the chain of testimonies, and the human witness to both will matter. The earliest and clearest theoretical recognition of the epistemological implications of the issue dates from before the famous "anthropocentric" passage in his article ENCYCLOPEDIE (H, VII, 212–13), which describes the sublime spectacle of nature as a vast unnameable solitude without man to order it. It is actually the article BEAU that first guarantees, with no proof thought necessary, that things have an independent, objective existence, but that their "beauty" (*beau aperçu,* or *beau réel*) can be appreciated only by *possible* beings, "des êtres possibles, constitués de corps et d'esprit comme nous" (H, VI, 156–57). The concept is weird and slightly humorous. Diderot is still so anxious to validate the world and also to make man its mediating but unsubjective witness that he throws out real men, who then race back to his sentence as depersonalized phantoms (transcendental subjectivities). But these phantoms will vanish too as Diderot becomes increasingly involved with sensualist and experimental philosophy and with relativist history, that is, as he grows— in our terms—more promisingly phenomenological. (In any event, as we'll later see, the problem of things-out-there and selves locked-in-here, for all Diderot's dismissals, will continue to ache subcutaneously.)

But what does it mean to witness? To describe. To represent. To imitate, and so to establish a view, an echo of the object. At the outset then, what we might call Diderot's creativity, as early as the Shaftesbury translation, and like Shaftesbury's ethical and behavioral version of it, hinges on an old and pervasive Aristotelian notion of mimicry. It is still, as with Dubos and Rousseau, symbolic recall, instinctive repetition of a presence or an absence, the playful alignment of an object and its duplication. But Diderot will, especially in practice, but also in theory (admittedly fragmentary), widen the classical and increasingly sensualized concept of representation to include not only the production, but also the understanding of texts and art-works, as well as aesthetics, in the Platonic sense, and science, as we've come to understand it since Bacon. In general, piecing theory and practice together, it can be said that, for Diderot, every thing, without losing its objective status, is summoned to being by its imitation, its interpretive transcription, so that one may speak analogously, say, of an "imitation de la nature" and an "interprétation de la nature." Diderot's examples are usually drawn from the arts. Artists, or authors for that matter, paint landscapes (among other things), which are not "la scène réelle et vraie," but only their "translation"—"ce n'en est pour ainsi dire que la traduction" (*Salon 1763*, A-T, X, 188), and other artists, witnesses, pick up the torch: "Je veux qu'un peintre, qu'un poète en instruise, en inspire, en échauffe un autre; et cet emprunt de la lumière et d'inspiration n'est point un plagiat" (*Salon 1765*, A-T, X, 393). The mimetic ricochet activates the spectator or reader to propel its effect. It takes place not simply, as E. H. Gombrich wants us to believe, between surfaces reflecting similar "schemata" or techniques.

Diderot, following Renaissance humanist theory, spiritualizes and deepens the exchange (as he had with Shaftesbury), so that beyond the text or canvas, poet and artist reach for "l'esprit de la chose" (*Salon 1767*, A-T, XI, 293), its concealed principle or inspiration. Yet productions of any type take on the appearance of double-faced mirrors set in a row, reflecting what is before them and announcing that reflection to what is behind—either onlooker or further reflector.[14] The evidence for this pattern is so abundant that Arthur Wilson's biography, by clinging to Diderot's own mytho-historic self-consciousness, his work on the *Encyclopédie*, the letters to Falconet, his frequent allusions to himself as Socrates and Prometheus (exemplary go-betweens), is forced to call itself "The Appeal to Posterity" and to act as the furthest relay of Diderot's own double projection.[15]

But there's more detail and enforcement of these theories in Diderot, beginning with the idea of inspiration. Close in this to a French tradition springing from Montaigne and an English one springing from Locke, Diderot makes inspiration an affair of the flesh. It enters

[14]In the case of a translation, for example: "Il n'y a donc qu'un moyen de rendre fidèlement un auteur, d'une langue étrangère dans la nôtre: c'est d'avoir l'âme bien pénétrée des impressions qu'on en a reçues, et de n'être satisfait de sa traduction que quand elle réveillera les mêmes impressions dans l'âme du lecteur" (*Eloge de Térence*, V, *O.e.*, 66).

[15]For a closer examination not of the structure of this appeal or "circuit of desire" but of its interpretive effects, see James Creech's recent article on mortuary joy, "Diderot and the Pleasure of the Other: Friends, Readers, and Posterity," *Eighteenth-Century Studies*, XI, 4 (1978).

the body, becomes the body's breath, undergoes an imaginative change, according to the "disposition de l'organe" (*Salon 1767*, A-T, X, 132), before being expelled. Like Montaigne's bee among the Ancients, the entire organism incorporates and distills: "Tout se réduit à revenir des sens à la réflexion, et de la réflexion aux sens: rentrer en soi et en sortir sans cesse. C'est le travail de l'abeille. . . . On a fait bien des amas de cire inutile, si on ne sait pas en former des rayons."[16] The merger of subject and object is so complete that, at a given moment, any referent seems illusory. Is the imitated artifact outside or inside the artist? Is he acting within his object or is he "obsessed" by it? "L'inspiré est lui-même incertain si la chose qu'il annonce est une réalité ou une chimère, si elle exista jamais hors de lui. Il est alors sur la dernière limite de l'énergie de la nature de l'homme, et à l'extrémité des ressources de l'art" (*Salon 1767*, A-T, XI, 208). At the furthest end of organic sympathy, advancing from passive reception to active begetting[17]—whether it is

---

Taking his cue from Starobinski, Creech deals very suggestively with Diderot's own ideas of death and posterity as they are drawn into a present, compensatory pleasure. How exactly Diderot sets up and manipulates his "posterity" beyond the confinement of death and even contemporary life—part of his need to escape any confinement, as we'll see—has yet to be studied, that posterity specified politically and intellectually, the historic reasons for and nature of posthumous sympathy pinpointed.

[16]*De l'Interprétation de la nature*, V, *O.p.*, 185.

[17]"J'avoue que j'ai beau m'interroger moi-même, qu'il m'est évidemment démontré, et par la raison et par l'expérience, que j'ai toujours été passif avant que d'être actif, effet avant que d'être cause" (Diderot's *Commentaire* on Hemsterhuis, *Lettre sur l'homme*, ed. May, p. 175).

a primary or secondary imitation—there is for the artist neither inside nor outside: he himself becomes that fine membrane dividing the two, sensing the two-way passage from one to the other, and unable to pronounce on their osmotic relationship. Memory, which ought to help reconstruct a separation or a sense of self, doesn't stir.[18] Instead there is the familiar hankering, as Diderot tells us in the *Eloge de Térence,* referring to translators (but the story, earlier recited by Dubos, is everywhere the same), to arouse "les mêmes impressions dans l'âme du lecteur" (V, *O.e.,* 66) —the reader, the witness, that "vous qui êtes le dernier objet, le terme de la composition" (*Salon 1767,* A-T, XI, 280). *Vous* arrives on the scene as an obtrusion of centrifugal energy, the surfacing of a reflexively inquisitive and acquisitive consciousness (*vous* is also *moi*) that has somehow, like the original object, to be tamed and yoked to the performing artist. (As Diderot explains the origin of language and its universal conventions, he summons up an image of a creature not merely blurting out sounds but discovering their effect on others, who instinctively "approach, draw back, beseech, make offers, strike, caress" [*Rêve,* V, *O.p.,* 279]. Every grunt is an act in a society where "there are only noises and actions"; and we know what we have said, indeed what we are, only after a noise or act echoes back.) And so the osmotic process continues, the author or artist swiveling from object to audience, creating

[18]According to the article GENIE, once thought to be Diderot's: "Le génie entouré des objets dont il s'occupe ne se souvient pas, il voit" (A-T, XV, 35).

new racks for consciousness and conscience. Is this why Diderot is drawn to and troubled by actors, artists who take on either the appearance or the inner reality of their models, who hawk their immersion or their hypocrisy, their insides or their outsides, for arousal? They swivel, apostrophically. Only the actor? Perhaps any of us, reporting, fabulating. The man, for example, who races to a public execution in order to fit himself out as a street-corner Demosthenes: "il pérore, on l'écoute, *pendent ab ore loquentis*. Il est un personnage" (*Salon 1767*, A-T, XI, 120). And Diderot himself, who, he says, learns only to teach, and who, upon reflection, but unaware of it at the time, hears, sees, reads, and thinks, only to convey and, in the process, form an impression for his friends (p. 115). Perception turns intentional; the audience and the object rush together and converge interactively within perception itself.

> Loin de tout homme public ces
> réserves si opposés aux progrès des
> sciences! Il faut révéler et la chose et
> le moyen.
>
> *De l'Interprétation de la nature*

Readers of Diderot collect and coordinate the patchwork of his aesthetic theory (or any other), as I have, and by coaxing these ideas from their literary casing, a larger purpose is lost. Diderot's project is not merely to pass along an understanding of nature and art in the linguistic flow of re-creation, but eventually to portray the understanding itself. With the result that so much of his important work willfully discloses the process of its own hermeneutic activity. Long before Bultmann, he suggests that to understand is to re-present and that re-presenting leads to self-knowledge as well as knowledge.[19] I am implying that

[19] It may not be excessive to conjecture that the Romantic renewal of hermeneutics stems from the nervous self-examination of Enlightenment aesthetics and epistemology, or that Diderot's groping imitations and evolving theories of imitation provide the clearest path to it. We tend to think too doggedly of rational Biblical exegesis and of the inroads of Montesquieu's, Dubos', and Le Père André's relativist explanations of artistic and historical events—as does Richard E. Palmer in *Hermeneutics* (Evanston: Northwestern University Press, 1969) when he says that "in the rationalist hermeneutics of the Enlightenment there is no basis for relating the artist's creative process to that of the reader" (p. 80). The display and the examination of a hermeneutic circle, the *process* of interaction between texts (or, extending this, natural phenomena, events, and artworks) and their "readers," a process so structurally and strikingly identical in Diderot to

Diderot's imitations care to expose themselves—a remarkable even an "unnatural" feat of reflexiveness, impossible outside the figurations of language, as he one day learned, while trying to surprise his mind thinking: "Il m'a semblé qu'il faudrait être tout à la fois au dedans et hors de soi; et faire en même temps le rôle d'observateur et celui de la machine observée. Mais il en est de l'esprit comme de l'oeil; il ne se voit pas."[20] The self, pursuing its witness, its outside, requiring its *vous*, another *moi* clearly, to complete its onanistic experiment, collapses into the impotence of solitude. Diderot's transcriptions (most frequently imitations of imitations) overcome this vacancy, the space between "le rôle d'observateur" and "la machine observée." If he were a painter, we would be discussing a series of the Artist and his Model, bearing in mind that the artist himself stands outside the picture plane, examining it with us. And we might in fact call one of Diderot's favorite strategies "perspectival" or "receding," taking shape in the Shaftesbury translation, and characteristic of all his translations and paraphrases, from *Le Joueur* to the deformations of Sophocles in the *Paradoxe sur le comédien* and of *Sir Charles Grandison* in the *Eloge de Richardson*. It figures as well in his articles for the *Encyclopédie*, which lean so heavily on Brucker and others, and in the modalities that control his

---

creation itself that imitation and hermeneutics converge—this is Diderot's unparalleled and unsung contribution. Understanding has already become what it will be for Friedrich Ast, a re-production, a *Nachbildung*, a memorative, expropriative poaching among the alien corn.

[20]*Additions* to the *Lettre sur les sourds*, A-T, I, 402.

Satires in the manner of Horace and Persius. It flourishes in his book or play reviews for the *Correspondance littéraire,* brilliantly in so small an item, for example, as his "summary" of Malfilâtre's *Narcisse,* and in certain aspects of the larger, more complex *Salons.* In each case we may, depending of course on our acquaintance with the original, simultaneously or alternately glimpse the object Diderot is copying *through* or in the interstices of his text or voice. The narrator-expositor hides his presence, seems, from one point of view, to be reporting or merely re-presenting, but he scores his discourse with a fine and recuperable tracery of interferences and subversions. It may be that only scholars, who have for some time been separating Diderot's overlay from its adhesive ground, can appreciate the interplay. But the fact that they have and do gives some indication that the artist and his model can come unstuck, that we can observe both. Some of Diderot's works are, in fact, structurally or rhetorically predicated on our ability to detect and enjoy his transformations, to assume a bifocal view of his text as a network of signifiers playing over another set that rises to the surface or sinks out of sight: *Tristram Shandy* in *Jacques le fataliste*—to mention the obvious—or an entire tradition of *impromptus* in *Est-il bon? Est-il méchant?* This may also be the case for *Les Bijoux indiscrets,* molded, as it is, over other licentious and picaresque forms. A half-century of extraordinary parodies, whose minor practitioners we neglect, no doubt prepared Diderot's readers for this subtler or more subdued bifocalism. By "readers," I do not mean to invoke actual or implied ones,

·though he could certainly rely on some of these.[21] Expectations of readers are, notoriously, shots in the dark, and the ideal reader hides, at times, even from the author. (Actually, he seizes the gun and shoots himself.) Let us be content to say, again, that the perspectival manner comes to life along a variable range of readers' perceptions.

A change occurs when the author, relatively concealed within or superimposed upon his object, decides to step aside and simply point at it. The artist now stands alongside of his model: Diderot in the margins of Helvétius, Galiani, Hemsterhuis, in the footnotes to Shaftesbury. A lateral or horizontal plane. We catch him less *during* an experience than *after* one, or, as often happens, the synchronic and the diachronic alternate in the same text, with effects that we think of as characteristic. And as this shift occurs, that is, as Diderot or his messenger steps outside his object, he faces us, like Velásquez in the *Meninas,* with a kind of self-consciousness that invariably frames the entire enterprise. Writing on Seneca, for example, Diderot opens the door to his reader and uncovers what we already know: "ici présentant au censeur le philosophe derrière lequel je me tiens caché; là, faisant le rôle contraire, et m'offrant à des flèches qui ne blesseront que Sénèque caché derrière moi" (A-T, III, 199). Diderot as St. Sebastian, paraphrasing and

---

[21]See, for example, his direct address to Grimm in the *Salon 1765,* A-T, X, 236. When all Diderot can manage is what he takes to be the mere description of paintings, he knows that Grimm is missing his "performance."

reworking Seneca, hiding, as he puts it, behind him, but also at times, speaking *about* him, facing us frontally, wounded in the first and third person. Diderot's consciousness, peering out from what was once its incarnation in Seneca, turns back upon itself, but only after it has drawn, or rather, threaded us into its arc. Now *we* are Diderot's object, promoted into censoriousness, yet asked to struggle free and become the close reflection of the consciousness that transfixes us. For a moment, we know what it is like to be Diderot's model, to stand between an unflattering imitation and a replica of his desire. Is there a choice? We're drawn through a textual voice that wants to be our own, to embrace Seneca, that other model "behind" Diderot, infused in his speech. Diderot's consciousness tries to recycle its outsidedness, objectified in us, back to the inwardness of mimesis.

The formula is complex enough, but grows even more so when the Artist's "I," which is, after all, launched in the temporal process of deciphering a temporal object (text, idea, event, character), changes dialectically in the interaction. It is relatively simple—taking more stable Artists first—to see him as the "lierre" to Batteux's "chêne" in the *Lettre sur les sourds et muets* ("S'il est arrivé à mes idées d'être voisines des vôtres, c'est comme au lierre à qui il arrive quelquefois de mêler sa feuille à celle du chêne" [A-T, I, 349].), first separate, then smothering the poor abbé, until no bark shows; or to watch him slip into the skin of a deaf-mute, once more experimenting on himself, ears plugged, at the Comédie Française. He opens the *Lettre sur les aveugles* by inviting the reader to thread a needle, eyes closed, like the blindman du Puiseaux; and later, pretending to "trans-late" Gervaise Holmes' fragments on Saunderson's death, he enters the blind man's world and speaks from within it. Both *Lettres* are especially interesting (though far from unique) because Diderot is concerned with people whose perceptions redefine the world in ways analogous to the distorting lens of the imitating artist. His Models set themselves up, therefore, as Artists of a kind, or, indeed, as embodiments of re-presentations, and in these cases, his perspectival mimicry recedes through two layers of discourse, texts about the handicapped, and texts by the handicapped. Yet he manages what I've called a horizontal rhetoric as well, placing himself alongside both, and in front of us. The examples are too numerous, but Diderot's *Salons* offer the best and completest guide, since he every-where invades and "translates" paintings and sculpture, from La Grenée's *Vénus aux forges de Lemnos* in 1759 through the splendid re-creations of Vernet's landscapes in 1767 and beyond. Most obviously here, we "see" through Diderot's eyes, whether he simply describes the scene or transposes it into its generic, literary equivalent, a dream (A-T, X, 396) or a *drame* (A-T, X, 335)—a verbal space to match a plastic one. This is exhausting work. Diderot, the organic filter, "sensible à tous les charmes . . . susceptible d'une infinité d'enthousiasmes différents," a performing machine, like Rameau's nephew, on the verge of collapse from imitative overexertion (A-T, X, 236). Yet, frequently, Diderot takes one step further and crosses the picture plane, or discovers that he can enter the picture laterally (A-T, XI, 199)—a "marche" he may have borrowed from examiners at the

Beaux-Arts, who let their fingers "walk" through architectural blueprints. Either way, the paintings swell to allow human entry, the imaginative scale taking its cue from the pictorial arrangement and its details, rather than from the actual size of the artwork. Man, in this case Diderot, is again the interpretive prism, the variable measure of things. Man or, rather, his language, since "plus on détaille, plus l'image qu'on présente à l'esprit des autres, diffère de celle qui est sur la toile" (A-T, XI, 233). No thought or language about a retinal image that doesn't transmogrify perception into a temporal and analytic enumeration that differs from the leaping, synthetic progress of the eye. (The idea was not then quite so commonplace, and even our structuralist or semiotic worrying of it [René Lindekens, Jean Paris, etc.] has added little but definition, guilt, and arithmetic, before or while slipping recidivistically into a "literature" of its own.) Diderot's language, nonetheless robustly, ushers us through the gallery or, really, a series of spaces whose common feature is their capacity to house us: "On monte vers ce vase par quelques degrés . . ." (A-T, XI, 196); "Entrez, et vous verrez à droite . . ." (A-T, XI, 201). Diderot, in the apostrophe and suppositions of the text, visible, between his object and his implied reader, Grimm, that other object, whom we are being persuaded to imitate. As he advances toward the painting or sculpture, he heads for its controlling principle—mood, action, object, person. One inch more, and he's not only inside the work, but winking at us. Reaching Falconet's *Galathea:* "Quelle innocence elle a!" (A-T, X, 221). A second later, he's within her mind: "Elle est à sa première pensée: son coeur commence à s'émouvoir, mais il ne tardera pas à lui palpiter." Or inside Greuze's *Jeune fille qui pleure son oiseau mort:* "Cette enfant pleure autre chose, vous dis-je" (A-T, X, 345). At which point in the mediation, as I've observed before, the terms "inside" and "outside" lose their meaning. Not only because, in these situations, Diderot's self-awareness flickers so rapidly, and our awareness of his presence with it, but because Diderot refuses to distinguish betwen subject and object. Here is where Diderot's rhetoric, like his style, as Spitzer described it, folds itself around the object in a quasi-sexual embrace, duplicating a reflected passion. "L'admiration," he says, "embrasse et serre sans réflexion ou la chose qu'elle admire ou celle qu'elle tient" (A-T, X, 221), like sympathy, "qui presse et colle deux êtres l'un à l'autre."[22] He is able, later, to tell us about it, as when, having described Greuze's girl throwing kisses, he comments (and notice how he assimilates the reader in the equivocal shifter, "*vous*"): "Et comme cette mollesse vous gagne, et serpente dans les veines du spectateur comme il la voit serpenter dans la figure" (A-T, X, 416).

For the most part, the *Salons* are highly self-conscious. If Diderot re-presents a painting or plunges into it, another Diderot is rarely far behind. These are, after all, reconstructions of things observed earlier, so that he cares to be the *sign* of a once immediate experience, an exemplary thermometer, interested and somewhat pleased by what

[22]*Essai sur la peinture*, V, *O.e.*, 700. See too the *Salon 1767*, A-T, XI, 118, for a reference to the same phenomenon in the theatre.

and how it now registers, in recollection. When, in fact, all he can manage is, "et ces reins! et ces fesses! et ces cuisses! ces genoux! ces jambes" (A-T, XI, 351), the exclamations and the sudden parataxis convey nothing more than an invitation to read the artwork by its (literary) effect, to imagine him as a reliable, affective extension of ourselves:[23] whether he wants to become Mercury and seduce Herse in La Grenée's painting (A-T, XI, 60), or replace Ahasuerus beside Esther in another by Restout (A-T, X, 167), join Le Prince's Russian baptism (A-T, X, 383–84), in order to grab the godmother, or be as lecherous as the Elders in La Grenée's *Suzanne,* he acts out his own, but also, and knowingly, our operative desire, which never takes things as they are. Inside the painting, even perhaps inside one of its objects, when Diderot appears to be most sequestered, he is, effectively, a performer—like Mlle Clairon, or like a child playing ghost—"l'âme d'un grand mannequin qui

[23]There is, in fact, a microcosmic illustration of this in Diderot's advice to Greuze for a painting to be called "le modèle honnête" (A-T, XI, 74): Put a figure of the artist, he says, *in* the painting; make him look as though he were filled with tenderness and moved at the sight of his model. The viewer will borrow his reaction from this artist, a surrogate of the artist outside the work. Only the moral specifications of Diderot's advice are new, not the concept of introducing the image of the artist in his artwork. As a practice in artists from Watteau, Chardin, and Saint-Aubin to Fragonard and J.-B. Hilaire and in writers from Marivaux to Sade, this image (often sublimated or masked) furnishes proof of an extraordinary self-consciousness at a time when old certainties, forms, contexts, and iconographies were crumbling. The artist either signals approvingly or simultaneously, defensively, playfully, or ironically indicates his own style of involvement with the new.

l'enveloppe,"[24] with an extraordinary repertory, including, to be sure, the role of pornographer and pornographic model. The reader's desire, in the largest sense, determines and yet is determined by Diderot's mimicry, which is, finally and inevitably, intermittently or completely, aware of itself as an instrumentality. "Est-ce que vous n'êtes pas las de tourner autour de cet immense Salon?" (A-T, XI, 84), Diderot asks Grimm (us). Whose fatigue? Diderot's? Ours? Grimm, as re-presented as any painting in the Salon, is pushed on stage with Diderot. They converse and end, in an echo of "Amen"s, by fusing identities (A-T, XI, 86–7). The reader, re-created as Grimm, that is, in Diderot's image of the ideal reader, with hardly any recourse, and perhaps even flattered, is slowly imitated, conjured away from his real existence, until, turning the tables, Diderot tells him, "ce n'est pas moi qui ai marché, c'est vous qui m'avez conduit" (A-T, XI, 89). The ambiguities of the master-slave relationship are already present in the *Salons* and, I believe, implicit in Diderot's earliest works. They grow rather naturally out of the processes of vulgarization, their real breeding ground; they simply become thematized later on. In *Jacques,* the narrator-reader relationship, in every way comparable to its counterpart in the *Salons,* doesn't so much duplicate as it inspires the manipulative dependencies of Jacques and his master.

But for Diderot's most brilliantly sustained piece of mimetic exhibitionism, an entire scenario, with prologue, action, aftermath, we have, finally, to thank Vernet's land-

[24]*Paradoxe,* V, *O.e.,* 308–9.

scapes in the *Salon* of 1767. Diderot pretends to be visiting the sites of Vernet's paintings, occasionally in the company of an abbé, who is overseeing some students working on a *thème et version* of Virgil and therefore, like Diderot, translating "d'une langue dans une autre les endroits qu'on entend le mieux" (A-T, XI, 107–8). The pictures supply such access to nature and its "accessory ideas" that Diderot bathes, as usual, in their depths and treats them as if they were natural landscapes. But in the "Fourth Site," Diderot, clearly indoors now, "dreams" or reflects in tranquility *about* the experience. Not the experience of reporting, but the presumably ineffable one of being alone, and ruminating, within his object, "le plaisir d'être à moi, le plaisir de me reconnaître aussi bon que je le suis, le plaisir de me voir et de me complaire, le plaisir plus doux encore de m'oublier" (A-T, XI, 113). Like God, he realizes, self-enclosed and self-sustaining—but unlike him in telling us about it. Diderot's memory is fixed on a canvas. His thoughts and feelings feed on the sight, but seem to spring from within, "comme d'un sol heureux." The forms of nature, actually nature represented, mediate the forms and content of his thought. It is as though nature, using Diderot as its mirror, had found its self-adoring and self-forgetful voice *and* spectator. Psychological readings of Diderot as narcissist, are bound to miss the point. Diderot reflects, and in full lucidity, the self-enthrallment of his object, and allows himself to speak for it and about it. He is still reporting. And, true to form, this loan or gift of himself (a "sacrifice de soi-même," virtue itself in the *Eloge de Richardson*), eventually seeks its witness. As if the existence of the report itself weren't, in this respect, explicit enough, Diderot, now focusing clearly on a washerwoman in the painting, whose noisy function it is to precipitate him out of the generalized haze of his impressions, reaches for Sophie Volland, his *vous:* "adieu mon existence divine . . . Qu'elle vienne ici seulement. . ." He's back, suddenly, to describing and critically noting how Vernet improves, aesthetically, on nature: we've passed, paradoxically, through art to nature and here, through nature, via Diderot's mediation, back to art. Then, finally, Diderot emerges, and as he does, his once solitary enclosure in the dream-painting turns into an existential solitude, mere creaturely loneliness, an expulsion from the promised land. "Pourquoi suis-je seul ici? Pourquoi personne ne partage-t-il avec moi le charme, la beauté de ce site? . . . Il me manque un sentiment que je cherche." He is eager to re-enact, with Sophie or with us, that earlier fusion of consciousness with its object. The metaphor is again more than slyly erotic. Only d'Alembert, in the *Rêve,* asleep and masturbating, duplicating the independent energies of the world, and ultimately, on the edge of wakefulness, reaching for Mlle de L'Espinasse, will again so successfully capture, emblematically, all the elements of the imitator's Januarian dilemma.

unstable and multiple I's

Modern readers do well to distinguish between an authorial voice and a narrative one. This kind of surgery adds another outside view to the film of consciousness that already lodges near the surface of so many of Diderot's works, in which consciousness ripples out from its own blind (unreflexive) center, each ripple taking its shape from a preceding and ultimately an original mimetic encounter. The temporal nature of this comes across vividly in *Le Neveu de Rameau,* where the "I" dances with its model, so closely at times that we can't distinguish between them, and the controlling narrative voice is, like MOI, alternately dazzled and aghast. How thickly layered and delightfully nimble this is! Rameau's nephew is, in every way, for Diderot, an object of predilection, an object in search of a witness. He is himself, of course, a self-willed imitation, a mime, a contrived presence, a spectacle, with the special, additional quality of existing in time as well as space. As spectacle, he typifies the life of the object, acting on the Artist, but only because the Artist, studying him, invests him with an imaginative life. The reciprocity of MOI and LUI, of subject and object, is such that the Model can be seen to assume the position of the Artist, and the Artist the position of the Model. All of this is spaced out in the time of a double mimicry, in a text whose theme is actually the ethics of mimesis or mimetic manipulation. MOI's outside consciousness, his *à parts* to the reader, is a continuous and therefore changing refraction of a light reflected from LUI, a creature part-real, part-invention, the product of his phenomenological commerce with the "prose of the world." Imitation in this sense inaugurates the very character of the nephew, and *as* LUI, a textual objectification of that imitation, it describes itself and examines its own operations with the help of an outside MOI. The furthest ripple (Diderot) has the least textual relief. It is, as Paul de Man might say, blind to its own insight. Having cast the first imaginative stone, it watches at a distance and seems only to record. Which is why the reader believes that every insight is his own. All the final, authorial consciousness manages dimly to register are the cumulative, repercussive shocks of irony and empathy that radiate from its narrator, who receives them from MOI, who gets his from LUI.

The temporal, interactive layout is more schematic, and so, less elusive, in *Le Rêve de d'Alembert,* its three parts connected or severed, as in classical dramaturgy (another allusive transposition), by the entrances and exits of its players. Each segment has its title. The first, an "Entretien," again specifies Diderot in his text and begins *in medias res,* with d'Alembert hammering out the consequences of some earlier statement by Diderot. D'Alembert is the sounding board, the contrived reader, of this Diderot's interpretation of nature. Like the nephew, d'Alembert figures in my argument as Diderot's object also, an interpretation and creation in his own right. The *entre/tien,* like all of Diderot's others, maintains a *link* not between two fully separable identities, but between, on the one hand, the artist and his model, and, on the other, the artist and his public. (The actual reader, as usual, is suspended at the periphery of the dialogue and gulled, up to a point, but never, of course, completely fooled, into throwing in his or her lot first with d'Alembert, then with Bordeu and L'Espinasse.) The "Entretien" is Diderot's initial *chiquenaude* of creativity: it illustrates the origins of an imitative process and sets up its repercussive structure. When d'Alembert abruptly waves goodbye, it is because he wants to sleep, that is, dream through the transfiguring contagion of Diderot's words. The "Rêve" proper, or second part, catches d'Alembert, all outer awareness gone, self-absorbed in appearance, but actually imprisoned within Diderot's vision, and deepening it, an exegete, lost in his text, and relaying, spreading its effects to further witnesses: Bordeu and L'Espinasse. Now d'Alembert is the artist, Diderot the object. Though the historic Bordeu may have instructed the real Diderot to begin with, he acts here as d'Alembert's reader, deciphering his dream for L'Espinasse. The chain of imitation, with its indeterminate inside and outside consciousnesses, in which texts are sequentially experienced and reproduced for listeners, until listeners solidify into objects to be read themselves, ends with Mlle de L'Espinasse, who, after several bouts of incredulity, so perfectly harmonizes with Bordeu that the two of them intone a love duet. The doctor trails off as she formulates and completes his thought, or their sentences chase one another in a continuous paragraph, broken only by the needless intervention of their names. These are in fact beatific, ecstatic, oneiric moments of "psychic fluidity,"[25] the explicator assenting and assented to; the listener not only absorbed, but inseminated. Which is why there must be a third part called "Suite de l'entretien," with d'Alembert gone. Diderot, who raced out of sight after the "Entretien," no doubt scrutinizes, as author, his final, worldly witness, L'Espinasse, who dodges the doctor's admonitions and promises to tell all: "je n'écoute que pour le plaisir de redire" (V, *O.p.,* 385). Their conversation hasn't been "sans témoin et sans conséquence," as Bordeu had hoped. (Can we trust him?) Its secrecy is strategic, a fictional recess, granting a privilege of freedom or license within and a privilege of invisible access to the reader outside—much as the illusory inwardness and privacy of d'Alembert's dream existed only to be overheard and bruited about. The dialogue concludes in an intentional haste and an utterly social wakefulness, fancy running amok, panting for a further "suite," a posterity among L'Espinasse's friends, and ours.

With the possible exception of *Jacques* and some of the *contes,* "Diderot"'s personal presence or his narrative "I" is missing from his other major fictions. Instead we get

---

[25] Herbert Josephs uses this expression very aptly to describe the erotic climate of "reactions of empathy in the exchanges of sentiments, pains, and even of powers" in *La Religieuse* ("Diderot's *La Religieuse:* Libertinism and the Dark Cave of the Soul," *Modern Language Notes,* 91 [May 1976], 748). It could be used to specify the nature of a good deal of Diderot's or his narrators' and characters' behavior in general.

surrogate figures heaped one atop the other. Disconcertingly the layers melt and recrystallize, the contiguous—as Diderot would say, describing his "grappe d'abeilles"—growing at times stickily continuous. So, for an early example, Ariste in the *Promenade du sceptique* reports Cléobule's mediative reading of nature, the Ancients, and philosophical sects. Ariste, the soldier, and Cléobule, the country gentleman, are so closely affixed that the narrator, in his "discours préliminaire," has to explain Cléobule's use of military language as an attempt to vulgarize, to level his discourse at this particular listener: "pour se mettre à ma portée, Cléobule avait affecté d'emprunter des termes et des comparaisons de mon art" (H, II, 77). Who *is* the narrator, Herbert Dieckmann wonders: "D'après la clé, c'est Ariste; d'après le sens, ce serait Cléobule" (H, II, 77, n. 15). Cléobule (speaker) and Ariste (ideal listener and transcriber) come at us through an interlocking and interadjusting rhetoric or frame of reference. The subject matter crosses a double threshold that Diderot erects instinctively and later tries unrepentently to explain. Does "le vieillard," in the *Supplément au voyage de Bougainville*, speak with too much civilized polish, the cultured elegance that A and B (or we) might use? Of course. Diderot, or rather A, recognizes, after the fact, that the old man's talk is "un peu modelé à l'européenne" (V, *O.p.*, 503). But then, the man's talk was recorded in Spanish and later translated into French. Are we similarly put off by Jacques' hostess at the inn? This too can be explained—if that is the word—in an afterthought that dubs her a lady and makes of her an avid reader, like us, addicted to novels, and so an expert narrator herself (B, *O.r.*, 620). But the *Promenade* has more complications. As Cléobule-Ariste enunciates the real and theoretical world, he clings equivocally to different and apparently contradictory philosophies (skepticism, deism, etc.), as if more than one spoke some part of his scattered, Laodecian desire. Desire, in effect, lights up unpredictably in the act of re-presenting its possible options. It has to be said that the world surrounding Cléobule-Ariste is symbolic and allegorical, more clearly here than elsewhere a text imagined by its speaker and yearning for explication and decision. The narrators collapse into one another, as I've said, but also into the texture of what they industriously perceive, part-natural, part-symbolic, indeterminate creatures of whom Diderot might say, "Je voudrais bien savoir ce que tu penses de ces gens-ci"—a sentence Cléobule-Ariste addresses to the reader, from the "allée des fleurs" (H, II, 149). They too must be read as incorporated adjuncts or complements to the monstrous symbols they themselves project and read.

For the modern reader, academically bred on the laws of logic and non-contradiction, this easy fluidity at the heart of Diderot's metamimesis is distressing. Either the subject seems to violate the object or vice versa; the narrator abuses some supposedly objective subject matter, or the subject matter tyrannizes its desirably stable fabulator. "Il y a donc contradiction," according to Jacques Proust, touching the point incidentally in an introduction to *Les Bijoux indiscrets*, "dans la texture de la narration elle-même, entre une tendance à ce que j'appellerais volontiers la *tyrannie du sujet*, et la tendance inverse à objectiver la matière narrative."[26] There is no particular need to invoke, as Proust does, the Chinese box construction of Chapters 18 and 19, both interpolations that probably date from the early 70's, when Diderot advertises narrative intrusions and constructions "en abyme." The rest of *Les Bijoux* is less Shandean, but not less parodic of rococo and older modes of narration, especially the supposedly "translated" chronicle, as Cervantes used it. It may in fact have been Cervantes, often mentioned in Diderot's earliest work, who offered a striking, formal precedent for illustrating the realities of interpretive approximation, the heroic perils of mimesis as incarnation of and incarceration within its objects. In both Cervantes and Diderot, fiction is built by the exposed effort of its characters and narrators, who weave themselves and their readers into its fabric. And in both, representation ricochets from interpreter to interpreter, as some initial object is read and reprocessed. Yes, one can speak of a "matière narrative" and of the narrator's attempts to certify its authenticity—an old game, but one which, in Diderot as in Cervantes, has to be played with the understanding that we are watching, in some penumbral darkness, always threatened, like El Caballero de la Triste Figura, by the withering light of detached consciousness, the *production* of that authenticity. An authenticity of imitative process, laid bare with the help of a narrator hanging on the words of other narrators. Tyrannizing subjects or objects? Scarcely a battle here where every object cries for mediation, and every subject, answering and hosting the

[26]Reprinted in *Lectures de Diderot* (Paris: Armand Colin, 1974), p. 218.

call, asks for the same. In the social circles of the Sultan, "des faits on en vint aux réflexions" (B, *O.r.*, 27). The "facts" in question are, at this point, revelations of the "bijoux," who speak, it seems, dispassionately and without prejudice (pp. 17 and 19), like any of the other "objective" chroniclers of the novel. Still, no matter how briskly or single-mindedly they translate their mistress as object, the object remains rebelliously elusive, and the message has to be decoded by outside "reflection." This is exactly the problem: not disbelief, but how to situate or respond interpretively to these reductive jewels (subject and object), who are instantaneously, fictionally "real" enough. The Sultan reconfirms his cynicism, Mirzoza fights bravely for distinctions and exceptions; they read one another through their responses. The Sultan's ring, which confers invisibility and access to truth (the jewels), may serve as metaphor for the illusion of objective inquiry or reportage. It forces an already fantasticated world to produce an oracular utterance from within itself. However invisible to others, *we* see the Sultan and the Sultan's magical will to make things perform. Doubly enveloped by a translated, "African" narrative that keeps him at the center of its web, entertained and enlightened by voices within voices, the Sultan images the artist, not so much tyrannizing as reflexively creative.

The term "reflexively" may nowadays be used categorically to deny the existence of a referent. Diderot and his surrogates would have thought this preposterous. The onotological status of the object as real, given, autonomously out there, is everywhere affirmed—which is what led

Proust, and not him alone, to notice a "tendance à objectiver la matière narrative" in the first place. Neither Diderot nor his narrators are half in love with Rousseau's "what is not." My point, simplified, is that objects, jewels, characters, fictional or otherwise, are posited with utmost liveliness and facticity in order to be witnessed; with the corollary that witnessing, inside or outside the work, brings these objects to textual and polysemic life. What, in this connection, could be more certain (objective) than a brochure called *Garrick ou les Acteurs anglais,* symptomatically retitled *Garrick, ou du jeu théâtral* by Diderot in a letter to Grimm (Roth, IX, 213), and about which Diderot had already written his *Observations?* We must attend to the nuance of Diderot's explanation for "observing": he says the brochure "m'a fait faire un morceau," as though he were solicited by it. And from this encounter two surrogate interlocutors spring eventually to question and be questioned, to sound off and alter the given "truth." They bounce this ball between them until they withdraw to their own, separate thoughts, not so privately that the invisible reader can't turn his ring on the mind of the first and more iconoclastic "homme au paradoxe," in which the ball keeps bouncing.

To the notion of "réflexion," which for *Les Bijoux* has to be taken in the Latinate and eighteenth-century sense of "le retour d'une chose vers le côté d'ou elle est partie," or, as we learn from Prévost's *Manuel lexique,*[27] in the physical sense of "toutes sortes de reverbérations & de rejaillisse-

---

[27] *Manuel lexique ou dictionnaire portatif des mots français* (Paris: Didot, 1755), 2 vols.

mens," we have to add the meanings of Diderot's use of "observations," and now: "supplément," since they all imply a recuperative project that recirculates and rehearses an object to its final exhausted echo. If "supplément se dit d'une addition qu'on fait à quelque chose, pour suppléer à ce qui lui manque," then the *Supplément au voyage de Bougainville* sets out to restore a significance missing but latent in Bougainville's account. It is an addition that enhances a thing by its interpretive "rejaillissemens," virtually replacing it—suppléer: "mettre une chose à la place d'une autre chose qui manque"—in its physical absence. A and B, the reverberators, closeted, sheltering their thoughts from society, but disclosed to us, snugly bracket the book they're discussing: the first part and the last contain only their conversation, and here they also refer to their own physical surroundings. They talk *about* the book, its implications, its author, and about themselves. It is as though they were dust jackets or end papers—an outer frame, conscious of itself and of what it encloses. We might expect that the intervening three parts would be a review of Bougainville's book, more detailed than the one Diderot first offered the readers of the *Correspondance littéraire*. Instead, each of these parts repeats the outer structure of the entire work, a conversation between A and B preceding and following a report about Bougainville's voyage. But these reports, introduced by the narrator, B, and called "Les adieux du veillard," "L'Entretien de l'aumônier et d'Orou," and "Suite de l'entretien de l'aumônier avec l'habitant de Tahiti," are in fact dramatized extrapolations, based on incidents and persons mentioned by Bougainville. Leaving Part I, which most closely follows Diderot's original article, its soberly factual assessment, its critical wakefulness, the reader suddenly sinks into a refabricated, fictional object. Bougainville's report, or rather B's account of it in Part I, is obviously unconvincing or unbelievable: "A. Est-ce que vous donneriez dans la fable de Tahiti?/ B. Ce n'est point une fable; et vous n'auriez aucun doute sur la sincérité de Bougainville, si vous connaissiez le supplément de son voyage" (V, *O.p.*, 464). Diderot now "supplements" Bougainville with verbatim reports that substitute dramatic and rhetorical "vraisemblance" for narrative "histoire," closing the distance between A (interlocutor and narratee) and his text by creating an imaginative recess within Bougainville and beneath the judgmental, outer support of Part I. These recesses lead to an historic present ("C'est un vieillard qui parle" [p. 465]), to the immediacy of recorded speech, or to descriptive passages like the one that pictures the arrival of Bougainville's boat, which moves from the preterit ("Lorsque le vaisseau de Bougainville approcha de Tahiti . . .") to the imperfect ("On lui jetait des provisions . . .") and finally to the present ("on s'empare des hommes . . ." [p. 473]), Diderot's breathless, disjunctive syntax duplicating the swift, successive activity of the natives: "on lui tendait les bras; on s'attachait à des cordes; on gravissait contre les planches . . ."

It is Diderot's purpose to force Bougainville's silence into discourse and image. Bougainville habitually says, to use B's words, "moins qu'il n'en pourrait dire" (p. 461). And the old native speaker in Part II, who in this sense is only symptomatic of Diderot's design and who, according to Bougainville, simply withdrew sadly and without a word when the foreign ship arrived, now overcomes, at its departure, his bitterness and contempt to harangue his countrymen with an eloquence borrowed from Diderot's own apostrophe in his first review of Bougainville's book (A-T, II, 203–205). The greater Diderot's intertextual liberties, the greater his attempts to validate his inventions—which is why, after the old man's speech, as I have said, we learn that it was recorded in Spanish by Orou, then translated into French, and that Bougainville, who had a copy, defensively omitted it from his report. Diderot's awareness of his own mischief invades the text especially at those junctures when A and B resume their conversation and prepare for another installment of Diderot's speaking fictions. B is holding, we must admit, an odd collection of papers in his hands, manuscripts of Orou's and the chaplain's transcriptions. Beginning with the close of Part II, B is both summarizing the chaplain's words and quoting them extensively, with the result that a prodigious feat of simultaneous reading and narration is intercepted by narrative dialogue ("La mère ajouta," etc.) and this by dramatic dialogue, with only the characters' names preceding their words. The range and variety of these repercussive insides and outsides, with their gradual to abrupt transitions, is remarkable. And there is even one passage (pp. 488–489) in which B summarizes a marginal note by the chaplain, the chaplain suddenly conscious of his reader, protesting in Ciceronian fashion that he dare *not* record the Tahitian parents' advice to their children—all of it spelled out in any case by B, including a direct quotation from what, one day, a Tahitian woman said to another. Everyone, in spite of constraint or privacy, is made to speak.

But the final, controlling consciousness of every utterance in the *Supplément* speaks through B at the close of Part I, when B, urging A to read "ce supplément" with him, says: "Tenez, tenez, lisez: passez ce préambule qui ne signifie rien, et allez droit aux adieux que fit un des chefs de l'île à nos voyageurs" (p. 465). The "supplément" in question is the one we have been reading and will continue to read in Parts II to V; the "préambule" that is "meaningless" is the section we've just concluded. Diderot ironically implies that the only means of "signifying" or scoring a point is by unsteadying and toppling narrative I's, by drowning exposition and expositors in direct mimicry—in, to take his first example, the old man's farewell. A line is drawn between reflectors and their texts, and at the same time, these reflectors, A and B, circulate in the very text, Diderot's *Supplément au voyage de Bougainville*, which they are reading, ensnared in an authorial net. Like a hand drawing a hand in a lithograph by Steinberg or Escher, these reflexive characters answer only to Diderot's creative and rhetorical impulse, which at approximately the same time, has been examining itself in *Jacques le fataliste* and will, shortly thereafter, continue to do so in *Est-il bon?*. But beneath this highest elevation of authorial and ironic consciousness, A and B go about their business in the interstices Diderot provides for them between his representations of Bougainville. They reflect, observe, or supplement until they have drained his fictions of their possibilities. All perhaps but one—which occurs in their last exchange, as the fog, suggesting the secret, sheltering caul of unsettled thought, disperses: the live, social "rejaillissement," the social and political re-enactment of Bougainville's conquered significance. The ball bounces toward the reader.

L'acte de généralisation tend à dépouiller les concepts de tout ce qu'ils ont de sensible. A mesure que cet acte s'avance, les spectres corporels s'évanouissent; les notions se retirent peu à peu de l'imagination vers l'entendement; et les idées deviennent purement intellectuelles. Alors le philosophe spéculatif ressemble à celui qui regarde du haut de ces montagnes dont les sommets se perdent dans les nues: les objets de la plaine ont disparu devant lui; il ne lui reste plus que le spectacle de ses pensées, et que la conscience de la hauteur à laquelle il s'est élevé et où il n'est peut-être donné à tous de le suivre et de respirer.

De l'Interprétation de la nature

It may already be apparent that for Diderot there can be no representation, no transfer of knowledge, without the intervention of metaphor or a metaphorical structure. With this in mind, one might venture three propositions:

1. Diderot's mediations form a "ground," a "filter" (Max Black), a "noeud" (Henri Morier), an "intersection" (I. A. Richards), between object and audience (inside or outside the work). They carry on a two-way traffic during which the vehicles at the intersection (text) take on a similar or comparable status: the target of the patrolman's, and one another's, intention. Without being metaphors for each other *stricto sensu, videlicet, rhetorico,* their traffic can be

diagrammed—in terms of their interactive commerce at the *intentional* level, the level of their intersecting ground— as metaphorical. Metaphor as metamorphosis: two terms whose qualities or actions are modified by the syntax that brings them together. (Let us think, to add yet another self-conscious example to those I've already proposed, this one revealingly autobiographical, of Diderot-Hardouin in *Est-il bon?* as such a syntactic ligature and prestidigitator. Hardouin is nothing less than the social projection of a literary performance: structurally, his "belles actions" parallel the authorial procedures of Diderot's "belles pages.")

2. To study metaphor is to deal not merely and stultifyingly with systems of replacement or substitution (René Wellek, Roman Jakobson), limiting oneself to word-metaphors and, at most, sentences, but also, and more dynamically, to study systems of transference (the Greek root) and conveyance, whole texts, for example, that act, as William Empson, speaking of tragedy, suggested long ago,[28] as vehicles for hidden tenors (themes, principles, values, etc.). If Diderot's vulgarizations nicely figure Janet's "panier" or carrying basket, his metamimesis, his insistent exposure of the project of representation, comes at us with the buoyancy of metaphor, of a tenor riding on the "panier," the vehicle of mimesis itself. In Diderot's

[28]*The Structure of Complex Words* (Norfolk, Conn.: New Directions, n.d.), Ch. 8, "Timon's Dog," pp. 175–84. Empson speaking directly of metaphor, Ch. 18, pp. 331–49, gives it the "pregnancy" of typifying images and generalizations, the third term of a comparison. His pregnancy is promising.

work, vehicles market themselves along with the imaginative produce they hold. The baskets too are for sale.

3. Mimesis and mediation depend upon images, images buried in language and those language deliberately evokes (things, characters, sounds, voices, etc.). These images act as vehicles that allow us to "sight" tenors and so gain "insight," to spy, beyond language, yet through language, a figured or "imagined" world—one that's made, functionally, to coalesce with, or at any rate, to tease the perceived world. Metaphors are lenses and so easily mistaken for eyes. Which is where the problem, for Diderot, begins.

The third proposition evolves from an eighteenth-century rhetoric of visibility, whose purpose, at the time— or so the theory ran—was to allow us to grasp one thing by means of another, more sensuous and therefore more "perceptible." The conflation of image, metaphor, imagination, and systems of displacement is Aristotelian (*Rhetoric*, Part III) in origin, and may be taken as an epistemological as well as a rhetorical axiom of eighteenth-century thought. To invoke any one of these psychological or linguistic operations is to yoke the others into its orbit. If metaphors are tropes, specifically, as in Condillac, abridged comparisons—"l'expression abrégée d'une comparaison"— all tropes are images ("Vous voyez que la nature des tropes ou figures est de faire image, en donnant du corps et du mouvement à toutes nos idées."[29]), and all images are metaphors for concepts. It ought, then, to come as no surprise

---

[29]*De l'art d'écrire*, Ch. VI, "Des tropes," in *Condillac*, ed. Georges Le Roy (Paris: Presses Universitaires de France, 1947), I, 563 and 560.

that Marmontel's article IMAGE, in the *Supplément* to the *Encyclopédie*,[30] speaks of an image as "cette espèce de métaphore qui, pour donner de la couleur à la pensée, et rendre un objet sensible s'il ne l'est pas assez, le peint sous des traits qui ne sont pas les siens, mais ceux d'un objet analogue." In theory, it is imagination, "la faculté d'attacher à un mot abstrait un corps," as Diderot defines it in the *Eléments de physiologie,* or "la faculté d'emprunter des objets sensible des images qui servent de comparaison" (A-T, IX, 364), that produces metaphors to sprinkle and reawaken the parched abstraction of language and thought. Diderot and his contemporaries never conceived of metaphor as replacing an equally "energetic" thing, since metaphors or images were thought to be cultural restoratives to a *"decaying sense"* (Hobbes[31]), latter-day supplements to an original, figurative language, now lost or partially obscured in metaphysical discourse. We have to imagine that, in the beginning, the designation of objects, acts, events, and mental operations, things seen or unseen, was a metaphorical imitation so loaded with sensuous reference that every word recaptured not only the things it represented, but also the trace of the analogical reasoning that went into its production.[32] Though freshly minted metaphors, as

[30]Reprinted in *Eléments de littérature* (Paris: Firmin-Didot, 1879), II, 262.

[31]*Leviathan,* ed. John Plamenatz (Cleveland: World Publishing Co., 1963), p. 63.

[32]"Il faudroit donc se mettre d'abord dans des circonstances sensibles, afin de faire des signes pour exprimer les premières idées qu'on en acquerroit par sensation; et lorsqu'en réfléchissant sur celles-là, on en acquerroit de nouvelles, on feroit de nouveaux noms dont on

Condillac explains in his *Essai*, and Diderot in ENCYCLO-PEDIE (both indebted to Dubos' cultural relativism), betray the progressive insights of a people, adding, as we would say, *parole* to *langue*, they are inevitably mimetic. Yet an unfortunate and, I believe, inoperative distinction was already incipiently being drawn between what might be called a heuristic or interpretive mimesis, and one whose purpose is simply to designate faithfully and statically what is given. This would correspond to the distinction E. D. Hirsch draws between significance (*signification*) and meaning (*sens*); between what, in this instance, a metaphorical mimesis suggests to a reader, disclosing unpredictable relationships that lead away from their textual support, and what it intends within itself, what meanings it unchangingly designates.[33] Philosophical rhetoricians, from Du Marsais to Marmontel and even Fontanier, defining images and metaphors, are so embroiled in the ongoing struggle for a universal language of adequate, accurate, distinct designation, that they invariably write strictures around metaphorical and "imaginative" usage—just as Hobbes and Voltaire invoke reason and judgment in

---

détermineroit le sens, en plaçant les autres dans les circonstances où l'on se seroit trouvé, et en leur faisant faire les mêmes réflexions qu'on auroit faites. Alors les expressions succéderoient toujours aux idées: elles seroient donc claires et précises, puisqu'elles ne rendroient que ce que chacun auroit sensiblement éprouvé." This is Condillac, in a chapter of *De l'art de penser* called "De la manière de déterminer les idées ou leur sens" (*Condillac*, p. 761).

[33]*Validity in Interpretation* (New Haven: Yale University Press, 1967), pp. 62–63 and 218.

order to restrict and discredit the passive or "involuntary" side of imagination. No matter how much the test of meaning seeks to remedy errors of mind and language by battening them down to sense impressions, the imagination, charged with storing and combining these impressions, threatens an idiosyncratic detonation. What Margaret Gilman and Rémy Saisselin after her[34] see as the rift in the century between a non-creative and a creative conception of the imagination, might be expressed as the tension between those intent on confining metaphor to its certain referent (meaning or sense) and those who depend on what new significance a figured language may generate: the difference, let us say, between discovery and invention, truth and prophecy, between reassembling a given world into linguistic intelligibility and assembling an iconic model or hypothesis.

The tradition of meaning (*sens*) acts like those panicky offspring of Pandora (Bacon, Descartes), who, having opened the windy box of metaphysics, recoil in horror at the linguistic chaos inside, the illusion and myth it witlessly blows about. Jacques Derrida is only the last, the most playfully ironic, of a robust line—after the Nietzsche of "Of Truth and Falsehood in an Extra-Moral Sense," after the Cassirer of *The Myth of the State*—its pungent flower, longing, after so much fertilizer, for an ordorless decomposition. "Like *mimesis*," he says, "metaphor *comes back to*

---

[34]*The Idea of Poetry in France* (Cambridge, Mass.: Harvard University Press, 1958), p. 29; *The Rule of Reason and the Ruses of the Heart* (Cleveland: Case Western Reserve University Press, 1970), p. 106.

physis, to its truth and its presence," back, that is, to what is given, so that "in metaphor, nature makes gift of herself"[35] —not to us, but through us, and back to herself. Metaphor and philosophical discourse, itself metaphorical and mimetic, create a dead space for themselves, a space of reference, "identical with its prop, with the governance of the idea signified" (p. 21). And when the sense of the metaphor is conveyed, both the sense (ideas signified) and the metaphor "fall unwanted and withered," since sense is itself nothing more than a metaphor for *physis,* unutterable, hiding its "essential or proper truth" (p. 48). Though Derrida and the eighteenth century, more sanguine or naive about getting at the "essential and proper truth," both ride along the postulate of the mimetic quality of metaphor, neither developed or, in Derrida's case, has yet developed, theoretically, the full ramifications of metaphor as a function of mimesis. The result is that Derrida consigns to a footnote "the question of this energy—carrying absence [metaphor], this mysterious break, that is, this gap which creates stories and scenes" (p. 40, n. 35). There is, he

[35]"White Mythology: Metaphor in the Text of Philosophy," *New Literary History,* 6 (Autumn 1974), p. 45. Though this essay appeared originally in *Poétique,* 5 (1971), I provide the excellent translation of F. C. T. Moore in order to call attention to the special issue of *NLH* called "On Metaphor," and also to set Derrida and Ricoeur on equal ground. The reader may also want to consult, in connection with the German tradition of metaphor, J. P. Stern's "Nietzsche & the Idea of Metaphor" in *Encounter,* 48 (February 1977) and the nice summary by Steven Ungar of recent re-examinations of the issue in *Diacritics* (Spring 1977), pp. 72–74.

believes, a "pleasure" involved—"that of the syllogism—to be completed"—which he confounds with Aristotle's notion of the spectator drawing inferences. But everywhere else, Derrida's metaphors are engaged in turning back, in knocking futilely on the closed door of *physis,* in using their readers mechanically and transparently to do what metaphors do—and, incidentally, to bruise their knuckles. Only Rousseau's metaphors, the nostalgic ancestors of these, do the same; but they're far more content to live *pleasurably,* in the end, within the "gap which creates stories and scenes," drifting bravely toward the future, in spite of themselves and of critics who stalk their non-referentiality, on the contextual tide of eighteenth-century hope. The linguistic theories of the two *Discours* and the *Essai sur l'origine des langues* surrender to the regenerative and now historic energies of the metaphors they create, so that it is only by attending too intently to meaning or sense—as Rousseau did, as Derrida does—that we miss their significance. At one point, Derrida warns that metaphors may set off an "errant semantics" (p. 41) instead of bringing themselves back to their object-referent, which is why "rhetoric . . . cannot be neutral," must try its chance on truth, that is, take its value or validity from its predetermined meaning. But metaphors do, in fact, shake loose from their anchor and have to be read, as any imitation must, glancing back perhaps, but more energetically forward, and not by eyes that move along as if attached inside the metaphor, but by eyes fixed in human sockets, and belonging to an independent, historic, interpreting brain. Metaphors may, indeed, be those ambidextrous marvels that refuse meaning alone and strike out toward significance, confounding both Derrida and Hirsch's categories with their functional, semantic ambiguity. If, according to Hirsch, "significance is always 'meaning-to,' never 'meaning-in'" (p. 63), never meaning proper, metaphor or language itself defies the territorial boundary dividing significance from meaning and poaches on both sides. The irony of Derrida's article is that, while it pretends that there is no foothold for discussing metaphor outside of a language (philosophy) composed of metaphor, and thereby threatens to paralyze philosophy itself, Derrida, like Beckett, allows himself to loll with self-indulgent and rueful *pleasure,* in the familiar, but here metaphilosophical "gap" of liars, illusionists, and metaphorizers. Even his metaphors express more than meaning and reorient us toward significance, toward *him,* toward *us,* toward the tradition he reinterprets.

To return, with pleasure, to Cervantes, who tells us that every donkey that reads gets his mirror image. Squire Quijana is not such a donkey. Those sensible creatures, the curate and barber, who read for sense and tolerate, aesthetically, the "gap which creates stories," burn the books of chivalry. But Quijana, the future Quijote, reads as though all literature were metaphor and sought not itself but him, and not only imaginatively. He does in fact get his mirror image, but transformed by the nature of the metaphorical mirror that asks not to be gazed at, but to be read and, in the process, to convert him into an extensional and effective mirror that tests the donkeyhood of those around him. "The result is that," according to Michael Polanyi and Harry Prosch (but before them, to Bachelard), "a metaphor, like a symbol, carries us away, embodies us in itself, and moves us deeply as we surrender ourselves to it."[36] Discussions about tenor and vehicle or subject-thing and modifier (Monroe Beardsley), the various anatomies of metaphor as rhetorical figure, all focus on the tensions created between the two terms, with arrows shot between them. The ultimate problem becomes how one expression can or cannot translate another, how or how much one ought to read back to the original or concentrate on its replacement or the ground between. What is lost, absorbed, changed? Like Proust's waterlilies, the vehicle-modifier is tugged back to its mooring and never escapes. Thus Philip Wheelwright, a New Critic, and therefore concerned with the autonomous "unity," "coherence," and "richness" of works, while holding that poetic metaphors generate new meanings, ends by saying that these meanings would "lose their identity outside the context of the individual poem."[37] Obviously we have here to do with the historic fate of reading, each generation modifying its view of metaphor to accommodate its faith or disbelief in the efficacy of literature or that displaced battleground for displaced persons, language. The stand one takes is in fact the stand toward which one is temperamentally and historically driven, so that whereas Derrida sees the cup of metaphor as at least half-empty, someone like Paul Ricoeur sees it as

[36]*Meaning* (Chicago: University of Chicago Press, 1975), p. 79; *Poétique de l'espace* (Paris: Presses Universitaires de France, 1958), p. 7.

[37]*The Burning Fountain* (Bloomington: Indiana University Press, 1959), p. 100.

more than half-full, and intoxicating. Metaphors are for him a new "event": "The meaning of a text is not behind the text, but in front of it . . . What has to be understood is what points toward a possible world thanks to the non-ostensive references of the text. Texts speak of possible worlds and of possible ways of orienting oneself in those worlds."[38] Ricoeur won't let himself be bound to discrete units of persuasion, petrified or even "generative" anatomies of linguistic surface, the sophistic, textbook sciences of grammar and rhetoric. Interestingly, as his article ends, he cautiously puts aside what he thinks this new vista on metaphor proceeding from its mimetic function will reveal about "the old problem of the imagination," which he provocatively says, "should be treated as a dimension of language" (p. 110). And a year later—a year before Denis Donoghue's *The Sovereign Ghost* (1976),[39] a sturdy rearming of the imagination against the structuralist and semiotic onslaught—Ricoeur's *La métaphore vive* enlists the Kantian "productive" imagination as a basis for constructing model or iconic images to sustain "la valeur heuristique des énoncés métaphoriques."[40]

[38]"Metaphor and the Main Problem of Hermeneutics," *NLH*, p. 106.
[39](Berkeley and Los Angeles: University of California Press). See especially Chs. 1, 2, and 5.
[40](Paris: Seuil, 1975), pp. 240 and 199. Ricoeur resolutely stresses the semantic, as opposed to the semiotic, "essence prédicative" of metaphor. He speaks of the "énoncé métaphorique" when he writes: "il enseigne quelque chose, et ainsi il contribue à ouvrir et à découvrir un autre champ de réalité que le langage ordinaire" (p. 191). And finally, for Ricoeur: "Cette aptitude au développement distingue la métaphore

Imagination crawls back through the window to rejoin its eighteenth-century family, and for our purposes, Diderot, to whom the assembly of mimesis, imagination, metaphor, and their prospective turn would have made good sense. Metaphors, more particularly visual ones, since these were considered the privileged children of the imagination,[41] are for Diderot the fine flower of language and thought. And like the sensuous world that inhabits them, they call for interpretation. It would be uselessly anachronistic to make a fashionable fuss about the sleight-of-hand these metaphors execute—the way, for example, the vehicle merely *suggests* a visibility and actually transfers the imaginable site of the invisible tenor (a concept) to one that is presumably analogous but no more visible. No one understood better than Diderot that if written discourse designates all visible things, "il n'en montre aucune" (ENCYCLOPEDIE, H, VII, 193). He doesn't wring his hands over the indirection of imagery of any kind, and this precisely because, first, he accepts the limitations of language as representation, and then because he concentrates not on the acknowledged loss but on the leavening

---

des autres tropes, qui s'épuisent dans leur expression immédiate" (p. 242). One of the few continental writers to appreciate the American contribution, Ricoeur promises to wrestle with the Germans in some future publication.

[41]In his article IMAGE (*Eléments de littérature*, II, 270), Marmontel, who is only typical, says: "La vue est par excellence le sens de l'imagination." Voltaire and Diderot both speak of other "imaginative" senses, but in fact continually exemplify imaginative functions visually. All of this is of course a footnote to Plato.

effect of representation: its having to be read forward toward other mental acts. When he says this, his point of departure is the commonplace comparison of painting and literature that Lessing will borrow, but it leads him to mention what he considers the "key" to language: its mysterious "compact" with the reader who has to work at revealing a referent that is always partially postponed, ahead of him like a promised carrot: "un pacte dont il faut que le mystère soit révélé; et il ne peut jamais l'être complètement, parce qu'il y a dans les expressions des nuances délicates qui restent nécessairement indéterminées."[42] And why is all of this situated as it is in a context of visibility, why does the genius who swells the bins of language with image and metaphor use his "*regards* plus attentifs et plus pénétrants" (my italics)? Because vision generates and regenerates not merely a figured language but vision itself and the concepts that flow from it. Diderot's confidence in imitative language derives from his faith in the visible, and this was not, historically, a faith easily won or kept. In Shaftesbury, who bears the burden of all the Christian millennia, the visible speaks for the invisible by stiff analogy. Its ultimate referent lies behind it, a moral, aesthetic, or religious truth that washes back to its creator. It sings the same metaphysical hymn to those who have sufficient grace to "see." But when, as I've said, the

[42] I'm still quoting from the same page in ENCYCLOPEDIE. The rest of Diderot's discussion modulates, typically, away from its point of departure to a more conventional discussion about the exact meanings of words. He becomes concerned with definitions, reason, judgment, etc.

world becomes for Diderot a "work" to be *observed,* knowledge of the sciences and the arts converging, as in d'Alembert's "Discours préliminaire" and the *Encyclopédie* in general, on the independent look and behavior of nature's or manufacture's parts, the visible loses its monophonic, its iconographic speech. Ronald Paulson describes what has to be taken as a parallel recoil from traditional pictorial iconography, one that "changed the structures of meaning in genre painting,"[43] and Pierre Francastel, focusing with habitual brilliance on Jean-François De Troy, notices "ce qui fut un jour nouveau . . . l'observation directe du monde extérieur."[44] The world stands disenchanted, a conversation piece. Whatever invisible concepts it hides have to be coaxed into intelligibility by the encountering eye, an organ so immediate in its operations that the mind can only later reconstruct its "visual thinking." We have to resist the temptation to call this "intuition" unless we restore its root meaning, one that only an age of sensationalism could have fully bestowed, granting the physical and not the figured eye its noetic potency.

Can the eye alone manage to grasp the world? Molyneux's question. Diderot's response in the *Lettre sur les aveugles:* yes, by trial and error it makes its way into space, the realm of the palpable. The hand becomes a "productive" vehicle or model for the eye as tenor, leading it out of

[43]*Emblem and Expression: Meaning in English Art of the Eighteenth Century* (Cambridge, Mass.: Harvard University Press, 1975), p. 104.

[44]"L'Esthétique des Lumières," in *Utopie et institutions au XVIIIe siècle,* ed. P. Francastel (Paris and The Hague: Mouton, 1963), p. 345.

confusion—even before the *Encyclopédie,* where the hand fashions its "métaphysique des choses," its own digital discourse, as Jacques Chouillet describes it.[45] The slowly practiced eye engages, like the hand, the geometrician's mind, the Encyclopedist's language, in an accumulative *bricolage,* probing the unknown with the stored memory of the familiar.[46] Diderot's premonitory genius in Parts XXX and XXXI of *De l'Interprétation de la nature* announces Rudolf Arnheim and upstages Lévi-Strauss. Conveying images to the dim space of raw perception, the eye formulates the empirical world into a set of working analogies which we call the philosopher's "démon familier" or the scientist's "hunch"—"Ils ont vu si souvent et de si près la nature dans ses opérations" (V, *O.p.,* 197)—their invisible premises, as buried from consciousness as these analogies are buried in nature. And now an interesting thing takes place: the eye's discovery eventuates in the thinker's "extravagances," conjectures whose analogical expression bears the formal imprint of the eye's divination. From the interaction of sight and the seen analogies bubble up in a weird "enchaînement," like dreams ("les rêves d'un malade"), a mad debris of transposed metaphors strung along an invisible generative premise. These metaphors have a tentative, that is, a merely cerebral visibility—"c'est un tout si précaire" (p. 198)—born of the eye, but only its

[45]*Esthétique des lumières* (Paris: Presses Universitaires de France, 1974), p. 75.

[46]See Jacques Proust, "De l'*Encyclopédie* au *Neveu de Rameau:* l'objet et le texte," in *Recherches nouvelles sur quelques écrivains des Lumières,* ed. J. Proust (Geneva: Droz, 1972), pp. 296–97.

figured reflection or mimesis. They become truly visible when translated forward into the physical world, tested in experiment, "les observations ou les expériences qu'on en concluait," *seen* again finally, but only visible in function. Observation at one end, experiment at the other, and in-between, thought—Diderot cautiously says "opinion"'—suspended on its chain of metaphoric displacements. There is no beginning or end. I round it off into a compassable unit, as Diderot does.

Metaphors want to function with true visibility. They have to settle instead for a kind of secondary or intermediate visibility, the eye's mind converting into the mind's eye. The advantage of true visibility is that it momentarily silences rational consciousness and welcomes trust; the eye is satisfied with its unutterable adequacy, sympathy, antipathy, and intention. No significance escapes. The mind, on the other hand, knows only by voicing its abstractions—its "sons abstraits et généraux," in *De la poésie dramatique* (A-T, VII, 333)—and can have no rest until they are rerooted in quasi-sensuous terms: "quelque représentation sensible, le dernier terme et le repos de la raison." In every other respect the eye and the mind chart a parallel course toward the truly visible, and for both, the journey out is also, in a sense, a doubling back, "la connaissance se portant de son âme vers les objets par le même chemin qu'elle y est venue." We know that they proceed from phenomena and go out toward other phenomena.[47] But

[47]Speaking of the writer in the article ENCYCLOPEDIE, Diderot says: "Ses idées particulières, ses comparaisons, ses métaphores, ses

they also selectively gather their sensuous past into their perception, the eye its former experience, the mind its remembered sensations. Historical and physical being so twine round percept and concept that a very personal eye and mind declare themselves together with, through, or in the objects they explore. Intuition reveals and metaphor visualizes not the object or the idea alone, but the performing agent locked in and returning its embrace.

This is unexceptional as long as we're unconscious of it, inside the process as writer or reader, propelled by its antic creation, cooperating with an imagination which, in Delille's nice summary: "Retrace le passé, devance l'avenir,/ Refait tout ce qui fut, fait tout ce qui doit être,/Dit à l'un d'exister, à l'autre de renaître."[48] The danger is in thinking about it or making sober "sense" of it. Only in retrospect

---

expressions, ses images, ramenant sans cesse à la nature qu'on ne lasse point d'admirer, seront autant de vérités partielles par lesquelles il se soutiendra" (H, VII, 192). More than a decade later, in the *Rêve*, Bordeu will similarly say: "Toute abstraction n'est qu'un signe vide d'idée. Toute science abstraite n'est qu'une combinaison de signes. On a exclu l'idée en séparant le signe de l'objet physique, et ce n'est qu'en rattachant le signe à l'objet physique que la science redevient une science d'idées" (V, *O.p.,* 369).

[48] From a poem called "L'Imagination," cited by Gilman, p. 101. To which one would like to add Diderot's own intelligence about the act of re-creation not being a regression or simple repetition: "celui qui suppose un nouveau phénomène ou ramène un instant passé, *recrée un nouveau monde*" (*Rêve*, V, *O.p.,* 269; my italics). The past becomes a metaphor in the present and so previews a future. This is why Diderot's verb, *recréer,* is in this context more emphatically hybrid than usual, suggesting re-enactment *and* fresh creation.

does the subjective element appear to have been gigantic, demonic, the entire enterprise, "un mouvement violent de l'âme par lequel nous sommes transportés au milieu des objets que nous avons à représenter; alors nous voyons une scène entière se passer dans notre imagination, comme si elle était hors de nous: elle y est en effet, car tant que dure cette illusion, tous les êtres présents sont anéantis, & nos idées sont réalisées à leur place: ce ne sont que nos idées que nous apercevons . . . Si cet état n'est pas la folie, il en est bien voisin. Voilà la raison pour laquelle il faut un très-grand sens pour bien balancer l'enthousiasme" (H, VII, 56). Diderot in this passage from ECLECTISME resumes a conventional orthodoxy and stricture, distinguishing what is "in" us from what is "outside" of us, adding his own little twist about being "in the midst" of objects. The danger then is, to rework a colloquialism, you are what you represent or vice versa, and what you see is what you are, etc. Getting and spending, receiving impressions and interpreting them or their re-created metaphors, everything may in the end be subjectively *ours*. Again the insidedness of mimesis, the dive into the midst of things, which is also a fall into the "deep well of the unconscious," surfaces to an outside that questions the waters. It's hard to believe that this threat of a colossal flattening of the world into subjective image is also Diderot's, but the movement toward significance, which is even more a practice than a fully developed theory in his work, emerges only through the fissures and inadequacies of theories of meaning. And these are full of bad conscience, banishing to the (subjective) dungeon of dream and madness half the imaginative faculty they rehabilitate.

Impressions taken in by the mind sit in judgment on other combined impressions, establishing a positive "outside" for themselves and a negative "inside" for imagination. And even the first set of impressions we call reason or judgment may be challenged as insufficiently "outside," as another radical subjectivity. The exigencies of meaning or sense combine with the skeptical interpretation of Berkeley's immaterialism and Condillac's and Hume's self-sequestering empiricism to hover continually near Diderot's mind, waiting for a breach. When this happens, as it does most dramatically around 1767, man falls away from the world, at least in theory; his eye becomes a stupid observer, registering differences rather than analogies; his imagination, a deceitful, unfructifying alembic: "L'homme à imagination se promène dans sa tête comme un curieux dans un palais . . . il va, il vient, il n'en sort pas" (*Eléments*, A-T, IX, 365). All the medieval and Renaissance commonplaces about imagination interfering with sense and judgment come alive again. How bizarre to see in that triumph of imaginative imitation, the *Salon* of 1767, statements like: "L'imagination ne crée rien, elle imite, elle compare, combine, exagère, agrandit, rapetisse" (A-T, XI, 131). Mental visibility and representation, severed from the harshly objective world, to which it contributes nothing but shadows, will have to be extinguished and replaced by the dumbest of eyes. An eye for an "I": "Le règne des images passe à mesure que celui des choses s'étend." In this kingdom no subject stirs except the computer.

A crisis certainly, as Georges May has said. But predictable, chronic, with episodic preludes, something like an infection at the core of mimesis, which is also the core of knowledge. Diderot is so wryly aware of it that in the same year he writes himself off as an irredeemable "homme à imagination," who could never find a place in the brave new world. Still, as early as 1747 or 1749 he thematizes the problem. And it lingers thereafter as a theme or implicitly as a disturbance in the act of imitation. Shaftesbury may have provided the topography of sight and space as the major analogy for moral feeling and knowledge, but space and sight are at least as central to *La Promenade du sceptique,* in which thinking is a metaphorical stroll. What makes Shaftesbury's world amenable to sight and then sentiment is that it magically invites those faculties to discover and participate in its forms and, in so doing, to disclose what is already formally present in themselves. We recognize this, *mutatis mutandis,* as a Renaisance space, "l'image d'une nature distincte de l'homme, mais à la mesure de l'homme et de ses réactions,"[49] a space badly disarranged by some modern interpreters (André Lhote and Pierre Daix, for example) to imply an overthrow of objectivity, with only a wholly subjective "oeil du spectateur" surviving.[50] It is in fact a transubjective space, which unites all eyes in perceiving a given world, the

[49]Pierre Francastel, *Peinture et société* (Paris: Gallimard, 1965), p. 212.
[50]Pierre Daix, *Nouvelle critique et art moderne* (Paris: Seuil, 1968), p. 46.

eyes and the world so implanted with the same divine or hypothetical principles that they exchange knowing glances. I have to make this clear because Diderot will remember and yearn for this transactional, relational space ever after.

Misery does then already begin in the *Promenade*. Shaftesbury's, and before them, Fontenelle's strollers climb or glide through nature and explain it happily. Diderot's Cléobule has the misfortune of watching other strollers and eventually himself among them. They walk down isolated "allées," occasionally stealing into the next. Hedges spring up or disappear, but essentially the three Paths to truth or God are separate precincts, limited and defined by what the strollers do or do not see. Their space is lamentably homogeneous and simple—by which I mean so tightened to fit them that they are quite literally hemmed into it. To have some notion of truth is, for any character in this bloodless and ironic allegory, to be trapped cruelly in the landscape he desires or worse, deserves. Allegory in its heyday was of course built out of an analogical concept of the nature of the universe. Could this be what prompted Diderot to make Cléobule, the neo-Platonic deist, construct it for him? If so, Cléobule doesn't succeed in projecting his cast of mind over it. For all its trappings, the *Promenade* works not as allegory—there is no story, no narrative development—but as an abortive metaphor, reassigning ideas and objects to a new space but clamping them down to their intended and univocal meaning. The reader is condemned to a "'predicate nominative' stage of criticism" "a sterile hunt for one-to-one relationships."[51] With the result that the *Promenade* has the dubious distinction of offering us a fine specimen of the bewilderment of demythified, "enlightened" allegory, a shrewd if unsteady vehicle for Diderot's intentions. Instead of narrative movement, we have a discontinuous, ironic frieze about which it is impossible to say whether a character's point of view determines what he sees or whether what he sees determines his point of view. And "seeing" here, in spite of the allegorical and occasionally "real" (purely fictional) geography, takes place almost exclusively in the mind's subjective eye. At first this appears to be true only of the clergy and the pious, blindly stumbling along with their canes of grace and faith. Ménippe sums up—actually, puts down—their predicament when he speaks of Jesus' contemporaries who had "la faculté de voir ou de ne pas voir des miracles, selon qu'il leur plaît" (H, II, 108–9). He goes on to say that other men "voient ordinairement ce qui est devant leurs yeux, et ne voient que cela." We're led to expect that some eye will make contact with things as they are. Instead we're catapulted into the philosopher's walk, where "reason" is proudly exercised: "Nous employons des raisons" (p. 120), and mortifying whips give way to geometrical figures scratched in the sand. (A telescope later appears, with no appreciable effect.) The deists seem to have an edge on the others, maintaining that "deux bons yeux suffisent

[51]Thomas P. Roche, "The Nature of Allegory," in *The Kindly Flame* (Princeton: Princeton University Press, 1964), pp. 5 and 31.

pour se bien conduire" (p. 117), but even they are eventually swamped in a reasoned miasma of *a priori* views. Skeptics (Pyrrhonians) walk into passers-by and rivers, bump into trees, tumble into ditches, mercilessly beaten by the author for their mentalism. The Spinozists, a confused compound of Berkeley, Condillac, Hume, and others, are called "visionnaires" (p. 120). Athéos, the atheist, comes out of his "dream" to argue against the imaginings of a clergyman; and in their hilarious exchange, which in itself assembles an ironic play on all kinds of "vision," from the physical (barely) to the beatific, it becomes evident that thought rather than sight is the issue. Enlightenment, illumination, reason turn out to be instruments of unacknowledged supposition, an "instrument inutile" (p. 127) in the hands of the Church, a plaything of the deist's "imagination" and his "yeux d'enthousiaste" (p. 130). The allegory of the "allée des marronniers" fades into a satire on the relativism of attitudes that rely more on conviction than sight. In a sense all three "allées" paradoxically connect, not because characters emigrate or hypocritically leap from one to the next, but because will, thought, and meaning, though different in their sphere of operation, function everywhere in comparable relationship to one another. Even the weak-eyed, sexy creatures in the "allées des fleurs" (p. 143), who find philosophical "reason" dull, exercise their own as much, if not more, than their bodies. Their "reasons" arise from other premises, nonetheless attractive to the sympathetic narrator who, falling into bed with one of them, encourages her to find "ses raisons meilleures qu'elle ne les avait d'abord imaginées" (p. 154).

The skeptic of the title must not be—though invariably he is—identified with the vicissitudes of sophistical skepticism in the text, but with an authorial attitude shared with the narrator (Ariste-Cléobule) only in the "discours préliminaire," when he is not himself in any of the "allées," where ideas, including skepticism and deism, are merchandised, outbid, or undercut. *The* skeptic makes his entrance through a vestibule furnished with busts of Socrates, Plato, Atticus, and Cicero, moves to an "enclos" of mixed topography (woods, meadows, gardens), and settles in a crossroad, an "étoile" of possible belief. For Cléobule-Diderot there are three available spaces: the geographical (the real world of men and manners), the analogical (Shaftesbury's "animated," "speaking" world [p. 76]), and the "philosophical" space of abstracting reflection. Insofar as the pseudo-allegory functions as such and winds its way along the lines of Diderot's earliest design—possibly called *Le sceptique ou l'allée des idées*—the first two are dropped or subsumed to the third. Cléobule-Diderot, like Voltaire in the *Traité de métaphysique*, searches for a space of judgment rather than physical vision, hoping to find "dans les airs quelque point fixe . . . d'où l'on puisse *leur* annoncer la vérité" (my italics, p. 78). Judgment, I can now explain, is one of Diderot's names for an outside consciousness that weighs two or more things; and I italicize "leur" to indicate that this consciousness may be an embarrassment, a consciousness spotlighted on a stage, self-aware before a crowd. But the search for a similar space of judgment runs through Marivaux, Montesquieu, and others of the first half of the century, so that the *Promenade* and Diderot himself are irretrievably entangled in the thicket of "natural reason," so close and yet so far from physical events. The unbroken tradition extends unnoticed, as a matter of fact, to Shaftesbury's Theocles in *The Moralists*, who has the same difficulty, looking for a "situation of mind," wondering "how to gain that point of sight whence probably we may best discern; and how to place ourselves in that unbiassed state in which we are fittest to pronounce."[52] Sight? In any event, what matters most pressingly for Cléobule-Diderot is whether statements about the universe are universally true or false—rational interpretation as Aristotle understood it in *On Interpretation* or, closer to home, Port-Royal in its *Logique*. The visible world is twice removed, flattened into a receding target. Both here and in the slightly earlier *Pensées philosophiques*, where Diderot, reacting to miraculous proofs of religion and so ferreting among the incontrovertible Plato, Cicero, and Augustine, could say: "Je suis plus sûr de mon jugement que de mes yeux" (V, *O.p.*, 41), judgment flies outside phenomena to "perch," as Rameau's nephew will put it, "on Mercury's epicycle," from which it passes sentence on itself and on other judgments. (Diderot's skepticism is not merely an attitude of mind, but a form of self-consciousness.) And because the radically subjective space of the mind's eye incorporates at will the here neutral, inert, and unassured data of sight, reason imagines it sees, and the eye is unproductively superficial. In the final analysis, all the

[52]*Characteristics*, II, 31.

characters of the *Promenade* are blind, immured in judgment and concept. Blindness, emblazoned metonymically in one portion of the text as the state of hindered sight (being blindfold) is hardly the invented metaphor we take it to be. The image is compelled and propelled from common usage, as Fontanier explains, a "métaphore forcée," with the abusive suasion of catachresis: "Aveuglement n'a dû, dans le premier moment, se dire que de la privation du sens de la *vue;* mais celui qui ne voit pas bien distinctement les idées et leurs rapports; celui dont la raison est troublée, obscurcie, ne ressemble-t-il pas un peu à l'*aveugle* qui n'aperçoit pas les objets physiques? Le mot *aveuglement* s'est donc offert naturellement pour exprimer aussi cette privation de la vue morale."[53] Language itself spews out the unsanctioned and banal figure as uncontrollably as the theme that figure generates. Diderot's characters fulfill somewhat somnambulent roles, resuscitated from their entombment in the cemetery of buried metaphor. Whence their pallor, their mechanical behavior, the exiled outsidedness of their judgments. As metaphors, they never speak toward the visible but back through shroud and shadow to a former life of the senses, the former life of language itself.

Before scrupulous readers, weighing the tone, the pros and cons of each sectarian argument to ascertain Diderot's uncertain preferences—before these readers pounce, let's return to the perfumed bedroom where

[53]*Les Figures du discours,* ed. G. Genette (Paris: Flammarion, 1968), pp. 216–17.

Cléobule in his wisdom, consciousness ebbing and eased, finally acts. We are here not to point again to the relationship of eroticism and philosophy, but to notice the cross-hatching of mimesis and the theme of isolated "views." Cléobule imitates the concluding worldly scene of the "allée des fleurs" with such relish that he dives voluptuously into his fiction, never to be seen again. What happens here occurs perhaps less obviously and with varying degrees of imitative assent or antipathy throughout the *Promenade,* from the moment Ariste and then Cléobule translate their understanding of the world and its ideologues. (Pouncing critics, as Gide would say, have made their choice.) But beneath and beyond the *ideas* it allegorizes, mimesis lays the ground for a theme of blindness and separation with which it struggles. Its distancing ironies would like to thin themselves out into assent, to shed the judgmental disease they catch from the visionary characters whom they attend. When Cléobule, the narrator-imitator, finds himself a blond, separate chambers or premises give way explosively to the pressures of a pent-up desire for relationship or fusion, here not surprisingly symbolized by a bed. A bed? Rather the imitation of one. Cléobule in love not with what he *thinks,* but with what he metaphorically, graphically *images.* The narrator in love with what he imitates; mimesis in love with itself. Cléobule spontaneously finds a solution (that Diderot often uses), not to Ariste's or his own skepticism, but to the outsidedness and separations of their fiction. Not a way out; a way in.

enclosures and exits

There's no need to detail how in Diderot's work, beginning with the *Bijoux*, a closed subjective space is repeatedly illustrated; how the judgmental vision of the *Promenade* becomes the restricted physical and therefore moral vision of the *Aveugles:* "Tant nos vertus dépendent de notre manière de sentir et du degré auquel les choses extérieures nous affectent!" (V, *O.p.*, 93); how blindness in its many forms modulates through the *Sourds*, the first and second *Satires, La Religieuse, Jacques*, and the *contes*, into "mots de caractère," biassed or uncommunicating sensibilities, dispositions, discourses—the various privacies of the self. Already in the 1740's it was clear that everyone had his "manière de sentir," and it's even possible to imagine that Diderot and his contemporaries were merely refining into epistemology, some into neurology, the lingering egocentric premises of Classicism, the deafness of desire in Racine and Molière, the single-mindedness of Leibniz's monads or Locke's *sensorium* or Hobbes's wolves. As soon as the handy metaphor, *sensibilité*, is discussed anew by Haller and Bordeu, something is confirmed rather than discovered, something ethically more ambiguous, irritable, and responsive, a new scientific context for the old model of "fibres" and "cordes," previously used for its musical and communicative symbolism by Rémond de Saint-Mard, Cartaud de la Villate, and Le Père André. But, oddly enough, the model comes to reinforce rather than alleviate the inveterate problem of claustration and its determinisms. Not surprisingly, *sensibilité* covertly leases the tiny cognitive and moral

81

space *sentiment* had earlier sublet to Fénelon, the late Nicole, Abbadie, Rémond le Grec, Marivaux, and to Diderot himself, among others. In the 50's that space is made more figuratively plain, and, as R. F. Brissenden says, its worth is assayed:[54] Clarissa shrinking into progressively smaller rooms and finally into her prepared wooden casket; Rousseau's sentiently circumscribed savage, a solitary virtue on the brink of distress from "causes étrangères"—moral paranoia its perfect spatial equivalent.

What is true of all these enclosures is that they seek their own transcendence—in the language of a narrator or sympathetic intelligence. They have their shells candled by mimesis and so seem to escape. The effect however is to stabilize these insides, to make them the prey of tyrannous, organic tugs from within and of rapacious outsides that force them into sacrificial retreat or equally sacrificial collaboration. Inwardness and otherness play a tug-of-war in which neither can be sure whether the tension on the rope is his. The boundary line shifts equivocally but remains a boundary precisely because the metaphors Diderot uses suggest a war and a victim. The self for Diderot is, unlike the prematurely posited and ghostly *je* of Descartes' "je pense," an organic structure reformed by and reforming an outside that fills it to the brim, an "être modifiable," perhaps, but at any moment predictable and, above all, limited. His theoretical formulations of the self and its

[54]*Virtue in Distress: Studies in the Novel of Sentiment from Richardson to Sade* (New York: Barnes & Noble, 1974), pp. 96–139. Brissenden doesn't spatialize as I do, and the examples I use are my own.

perceptions, beginning with the *Aveugles,* increasingly concentrate on the two-way tug, with some sort of transcendent referee or judgmental self standing above and describing the battle. Between the "Lettre à Landois" (1756) in which our motivation "nous est toujours extérieur, étranger, attaché ou par une nature ou par une cause quelconque, qui n'est pas nous" (Roth, II, 207), and the *Commentaire d'Hemsterhuis* (1773 – 74) in which "tout motif, soit qu'il nous soit extérieur ou intérieur est indépendant de nous," there may be a subtle switch of emphasis from external impingements to internal "causes propres à l'homme,"[55] but Diderot's *nous* remains, conceptually and emblematically, in both sentences, a nebulous and dislocated consciousness, somewhere outside the self it predicates— the self to which things happen or from which they proceed. He doesn't try to explain this *nous,* withdrawn miraculously and metaphorically from the self's subjectivity to act as its double, but as a free agent whose surveillance only language, not sense, allows. Yet it intimates in its transcendence[56] and assembled persistence that the performing (writing) self has resources independent of the problem it scans and doesn't logically solve.

[55]Ed. G. May, p. 173; Jacques Chouillet, "Des causes propres à l'homme," in *Approches des lumières: mélanges offerts à Jean Fabre* (Paris: Klincksieck, 1974), pp. 53 – 62.

[56]I use the term transcendence here and a bit later to refer to a trans-subjective "nous" and "je." I ought to make it clear, since Jean-François Lyotard, in his superb *Discours, figures* (Paris: Klincksieck, 1974), is troubled by the depersonalized, unhistoric "On" of phenomenological analysis, that it is possible for "on," "nous," or "je" (even in the

The tug, then, lasts. Whose victim is Rameau's nephew, Mlle de la Chaux, Jacques, Mme de la Pommeraye, Hardouin? The answer in the case of Suzanne is less ambiguous only because claustration is literally translated into imprisonment. But notice what happens to the poet, the artist, in *Le Paradoxe,* where the tug, as we know, is at its fiercest. *Sensibilité,* activated in part by a lively (passive) imagination, has now the effect of trapping the person wholly within himself, "à moins qu'il ne puisse s'oublier et se distraire de lui-même" (A-T, VIII, 408). Unless, that is, he's able to find some outside "modèle" to catch hold of. And what can piece together this model? A homeopathic "imagination forte"—an active, willful imagination, but here reduced simply to rearranging shards of received impressions. In which case, as Diderot puts it, "ce n'est plus lui [the thinker] qui agit, c'est l'esprit d'un autre qui le domine." At this point Diderot isn't speaking about actors, who have their roles cut out for them, so that the more one thinks of it, the more puzzling this "esprit d'un autre" becomes; until one understands it as a metaphor for outsidedness—in this instance, a deliberate distancing from the physical and affective self inspired by the anxiety

---

general sense in which Merleau-Ponty uses these pronouns) to express an individual condition, Lyotard's "Ça du désir" (p. 23), and still unload a generality, as Lyotard's own pronouns knowingly and ironically do. In the case of Diderot, "nous" or "je" can, as I am suggesting, and precisely because of the rhetorical figures whose freedom Lyotard defends, establish a second center for itself, a displaced, sublimated, but still articulate center, an "It" (Groddeck's equivalent of "Ça") in the midst of a generalized discourse.

of self-restriction and, paradoxically, as victimizing as the self from which it escapes. As Diderot theorizes, but only as he theorizes and illustrates his theory, the gap between inside and out, self and world, between the given and the created, and between the two imaginations (passive and active), widens and congeals. On either side the space is similarly closed, unmastered, and hostile.

Earlier, however, Rameau's nephew and MOI, in the masterful example of semantic and conceptual misprisions we call their "dialogue," shuttled between these spaces. But what *Le Neveu* actually disclosed, in spite of the separations it intended to illustrate, and still does, is how hopeless it is to draw a line between heredity and acquired experience, between what is given to us from the inside and the outside, and between these and conscious self-projection—what we determinedly *make* of the given. The self here, like Rousseau's statue of Glaucus, is somehow coextensive with its surrounding encrustations. It searches for its authentic face, its unity, among the accretions that form it and continue to deposit their sediment. Its effort, its imagination—in which Maine de Biran will later see the evidence of a free and true self—plays in the dust, modeling momentary profiles and performances, proving, in spite of the indistinguishable materials of the given and the adventitious, that there is once again an epiphenomenal "I" to stand partially above and outside determinisms and enclosures. MOI only most dramatically through his reportage, and LUI through his mimes and stories, transcend the limits of the selves they speak about. But this is not simply transcendence. If they escape from their personal and ideological frames, even take positions at the other end of the rope, it's because they can interact imitatively, collaborate on their own terms, that is, phenomenologically, with the opposition, give and take until the gap, the problem of boundaries, is reduced to mere "outside" (our) speculation.

The escape from Diderot's problem of blindness, division, and impotence, as well as from the multiplicities and contradictions of consciousness, which become more strident or aggravated with age and analysis, is written, often blindly, into his work—or the work of his narrators and protagonists. One might say that these works present, in Emerson's phrase, "a solution in hieroglyphic to those inquiries he would put." Diderot reactivates in his worry and implicitly in his claustrophobia and digressive style[57]

---

[57] A discussion of Diderot's style, especially of its digressiveness, and of the eccentric "unity" of his texts would lead me far afield. Yet coming at the issues in this context and, biographically, in the context of Diderot's "tendency to suffer from claustrophobia which many critics have failed to mention" (Otis Fellows, *Diderot* [Boston: Twayne Publishers, G. K. Hall & Co., 1977], p. 52) may yield a new perspective. The most sustained studies of Diderot's digressions, Georges May's "Diderot, Artiste et Philosophe du Décousu," in *Europäische Aufklärung*, eds. H. Friedrich and F. Schalk (Munich: Wilhelm Fink, 1967) and David Berry's *The Technique of literary digression in the fiction of Diderot*, in *Studies on Voltaire and the Eighteenth Century*, 118 (Banbury, Oxfordshire: Cheney & Sons, Ltd., 1974), deal with the suitability of style to content, Diderot's search, in Herbert Dieckmann's terms (*Cinq leçons sur Diderot* [Geneva and Paris: Droz and Minard, 1959], p. 82), for a "natural" and necessarily unorthodox expression, a mimetic correspondence between the structure or movement of his mind and his hectic, atomistic vision of

the themes of confinement to be found in the early century, from Montesquieu and Marivaux through Voltaire and Vauvenargues, and, on occasion, the social and political realities that urged them into being. But more of these themes later. For the moment, they have to be seen not so much as the background as the thicket through which Diderot or his characters struggle toward a clearing, not an empty space, but a space of possible encounter and *relationship,* where transactions are mimetic. Saunderson's blunted life, a "long désir" and a "privation continuelle," is rescued

the universe. May's elegant descriptions and documentation suggest more than what his conclusions make of them: he speaks of Diderot as an "écrivain de l'inachevé," of his contempt for completed "books," and of Diderot's own association of madness and dream with the "unknitted" style. A finished, architectonic discourse is also a rational box. It is not only a matter of escaping from Classical rhetoric and of finding an adequate, independent speech (which cannot in any case highlight the specificity of Diderot in his century), but of not succumbing to one's own. Diderot's digressions break out of a foreseeable container and create a double presence, one sensed as claustrophobically written or to be written, the other as escaped, free to diverge, survey, or overreach—in a moment he himself calls "repose." Even this centrifugal energy, however, when after its deed it names or acknowledges itself, may seem to have been an imprisoning vortex, Diderot or his narrator then turning for "repose" not to a stylistic deviation or "écart" but to a new reader, another level of being and consciousness, or to the airy "repose" of acknowledgement, consciousness itself. "To be myself completely," as Diderot once put it, is actually therefore to be not, at that instant, what he has been, stylistically, rhetorically—with all this implies of an orientation of consciousness. Plentiude or freedom exists diacritically, in opposition to what has transpired or is bound to transpire, and is neither a content nor a specific state of mind: all movements of his pen draw a by his educated guess about the fermentation of matter and its oceanic evolution. Like Theocles or Cléobule, he needs some foothold outside his physical limits, and, incidentally, he also needs company: "Transportez-vous avec moi sur les confins de cet univers, au-delà du point où je touche" (V, *O.p.*, 123). But he finds it neither in the conventional space of purely judgmental and rational exchange nor in the constrictions of the subjective senses, but in an intermediate area of metaphoric vision. He might have said, along with the Diderot of the *Lettre sur les sourds:*

---

square, an inside, whether we, glorifying his open-endedness, see one or not. The "folie" and the oneiric quality of the centrifugal presence are indeed *mad*ness: a revenge taken against the threat of suffocation and constriction (domination), whether self-imposed or imposed by a real or imaginary otherness. It is as if Diderot makes plans (for plays, books, and even personal involvements) and in fact writes or enacts some of these in order, at times, to enjoy the pleasure and relief of evasion— finally, or in the interstices of his act: the pent-up, even prepared pleasure of frustrating and releasing their (his) hold on him(self). This is, I believe, the true meaning of Starobinski's "aliénation consentie" (see note 11) and of Diderot-Hardouin's mischievous retaliations in *Est-il bon?*. The defeat of linear expectation or of what we might call realization is scored with a double-edged sword that strikes the author along with his objects, friends, and readers. The reader can recuperate both the potential realization or direction and its subversion in a single work, and not only in its style but, as we'll see, in its structure, most obviously with the help of Diderot's extraordinary frames (those for example of *Le Fils naturel* and *La Religieuse*) that demolish an intention while providing a window on it. One can view, with Berry, the digressions in *Jacques* as an "artistic technique" (p. 261), merely mimetic, while also viewing them as triumphant, ironic, and self-conscious examinations of what had always been Diderot's claustrophobic scriptural behavior.

"notre imagination est moins scrupuleuse que nos yeux" (A-T, I, 404). Metaphor and visibility here again, but not simply as the latent condition of things and language, that is, as significance, the measure of our receptivity and contribution, but as release, the unification of consciousness into a wedge against darkness. And with this added power: the ability to create *within* the space it gains and then mimetically frames, a unity so compelling that it draws assent and absorbs its witnesses.[58] Suzanne no longer alone, at least momentarily, as she writes to the marquis de Croismare; Jacques telling his tales and so linked complicitously with his fascinated master, Rameau's nephew with MOI and the onlookers at the café de la Régence, Diderot with his reader.

Loneliness overcome. If every sequestered inside longs to climb out, and every outside (witness or consciousness) to climb in, the coveted space has to dispel loneliness, set perception into a world it can assemble around it. Diderot welcomes therefore any natural or mimetic principle—even to the light and air that fuse color on a painting's surface—that binds or combines, that rivets attention and makes it slide effortlessly and whole between

[58] Again William Empson can be enlisted: "The peculiar absorption of consciousness during orgasm (the collapse of one's everyday mental connections) seems to be the basis of the first shock of metaphor" (*Complex Words*, p. 349). The sexual metaphor is stunningly apposite; "the collapse of one's everyday mental connections" also suggests, I think, what Coleridge would have called the "somnial magic" of the connections the mind does, in this condition, make. As in dreamwork, the mind sets itself within the connections it frames.

objects, that gives the self or the eye its capacity to be *with* things, *according to* things, as Merleau-Ponty says,[59] and yet remain itself, with its own integrity or "unité de caractère." No one and no thing need stand alone, unembraced by perception and transcription, by an encyclopedic web of analogy and family resemblance. At the moment of perception and transcription, insides reach toward outsides and coalesce with them, or vice versa. "Analogies," "rapports," "idées accessoires," those terms every reader of Diderot watches him rehearse as early as Shaftesbury's essay, and thereafter in the *Mémoires de mathématiques,* the article BEAU, the *Lettre sur les sourds,* the *Salons* (of 1765 and 1767 especially), the *Essai sur la peinture,* are wrapped in desire and self-fulfilling intention—a "sentimental" intention, as I'll later explain—which is why, in Diderot's case, we're forced to make such a fuss over terms that were already standard in aesthetics, law, science, and religion. It's their intention or desire that establishes a distinction, actually a hierarchy, among sought-after effects within the class of perceptual connections, among, for example, the "grossières analogies" Diderot detects in C. Van Loo's *Vestale* or Servandoni's ruins (A-T, X, 252 and 308) and those other "analogies fines et déliées qui appellent sur la toile les objets les uns à côté des autres et qui les y lient par des fils secrets et imperceptibles" (A-T, X, 257). Not that

[59]"Je serais bien en peine de dire *où* est le tableau que je regarde . . . je ne le fixe pas en son lieu, mon regard erre en lui comme dans les nimbes de l'Etre, je vois selon ou avec lui plutôt que je ne le vois" (*L'Oeil et l'esprit* [Paris: Gallimard, 1964], p. 23).

Diderot can't appreciate the first sort. He can even propose, in the *Essai sur la peinture* (V, *O.e.*, 708–9), a painting in which all objects (a hut, a tree, a man) are similar in look and signal, "gross" in their discursive relationship and message: the artist intends a concept and his painting translates back to one. We're not far from cardboard allegory or from certain aspects of rococo aesthetics in which mental "liaisons" and "idées accessoires" provide those solitary and withdrawn "plaisirs de l'âme" the artist expects us to compose for ourselves. The mind, once sparked, is free to wander off on a current of Lockean associations, since, as Montesquieu put it, "toutes les choses sont dans une chaîne."[60] "Grossières analogies" are therefore only halfway stations to "analogies fines et déliées," analogies that not only "tie" objects together and in place, but stun and prolong feeling, inducing the mind not to leap but to be cradled within the harmony of its objects.

Language itself demands its release and comfort too. In my last epigraph, it scales solitary mountains "dont les sommets se perdent dans les nues," leaving the long-distance speaker with the loneliness of "la conscience de la hauteur à laquelle il s'est élevé." It can attract company only by reintroducing "les objets de la plaine." Once ascended, it looks wistfully back—through metaphor, as we know,—or, in the *Lettre sur les sourds,* once more inscribed in a context of solitude, through gestural signs and poetry's "hieroglyphics," which is to say, the same

[60]*Essai sur le goût* in *Oeuvres complètes,* ed. Roger Caillois (Paris: Gallimard, 1958), II, 1243.

thing: "combien la langue des gestes est métaphorique!" (A-T, I, 356). The new rapprochement Diderot proposes in the *Lettre* involves not only the deaf but society in general, which he pictures as an assortment of people deprived of all but one sense organ (not the same one!), "ce qui arrive à tout moment dans le monde" (p. 353). They're able to communicate through the conventional signs of geometry alone. Gestures and poetry may get them out of this bind: they link expression to thought and feeling instantly, capture not discursively but presentationally, in Susanne Langer's sense, "une seule vue de l'âme" (p. 367), a synchrony, "un tableau," a cohesion of impressions "en entier, et tout à la fois" (p. 369). What the spectator or reader "sees" with untranslatable, that is, only interpretive immediacy, even if he has no eyes or ears, are metaphors for concepts and their accompanying feeling, formalized signs of such fused density that no shadow falls between spirit and matter, perceiver and the thing signified. Responding to the objections of the *Journal de Trévoux,* Diderot explains, in Augustinian terms the editors would have approved, that the words of conventional language "ne sont que les signes de nos idées" (p. 414), just as later on in the *Paradoxe* he'll say that "les mots ne sont et ne peuvent être que des signes approchés d'une pensée, d'un senti- ment, d'une idée" (V, *O.e.,* 304)—all of which makes them counters for subjective and cultural misunderstandings. They gambol in the chancy fields of meaning (*sens*) where value can be found only in sunny definitions. But gesture and poetry draw us through their very forms into an irresistible empathy.[61] This may be Diderot's covert and paradoxical contribution to the pursuit of a universal language, a discourse for the handicapped (all of us), an "ordre naturel des idées et des signes" (p. 364) that stretches from the unlettered gesture to the poetic and "sublime" statement. Lady Macbeth, silent, eyes closed, rubbing out the damned spot—"Quelle *image* du remords!" (p. 355; my italics). Lucretius, Virgil, Voltaire, Boileau, spinning their "tissu d'hiéroglyphes" (p. 374), making imaginatively sensuous forms so that "dans le même temps que l'entendement les saisit, l'âme en est émue, l'imagination les voit et l'oreille les entend." The indivisibilities of gesture and poetry, packaging together meaning and sense impressions, fusing sign and thought, the visible and invisible, flashing plenitude out of the linearity of language, assembles—one might say, eases—consciousness by mirroring and connecting its diffuse attentions.

The mimetic "ordre naturel des idées et des signes" calls for an extraordinary effort of reintegration, an effort at relaxation into supposedly primitive, pre-linguistic acts, that seems to contradict the "natural," effortless qualities of the metaphoric activity it hopes to produce. This is because Diderot's "nature" and "ordre naturel," like his primitivism

[61]I take this to be Diderot's meaning in the *Eloge de Térence* when, in discussing the indivisibility of form and content, he says: "quand le style est bon, il n'y a point de mot oisif; et qu'un mot qui n'est pas oisif représente une chose" (V, *O.e.*, 65). It goes without saying that once the "thing" receives its hypotyposis, its sensuous form, it draws our collaborative response.

or Neo-Classicism in general, are themselves metaphors that intersect in the present, but point to the past and more strenuously to a future. They musn't be taken literally; they never completely touch ground, but inch toward reform, like that other generative metaphor, the "modèle idéal," a collective, historic striving toward something that never was and never could be fully realized. To invoke natural signs, a natural "ordre d'idées préexistant dans son esprit, tout contraire à celui des expressions," or natural modes of behavior, is to align oneself with an historic, paradigmatic effort to recapture contact with one's ideas, one's body, language, and society. In the beginning, that is to say, was not metaphor, but those feelings of immediacy and relationship that metaphoric signs or representations sprang up to communicate—redemptively, already looking behind, but with salvation necessarily in what they promised on ahead. And in heightened moments, when relationship is transubstantiated, created or experienced like a symbolic wafer, nature seems to speak or is made to speak again.

representation as repetition

I take this in fact to be the major supposition of Dorval's play, *Le Fils naturel:* the very facticity of the world, of every inner or outer event (no absolute distinction possible here), would slip away without its transubstantiation. If we watch it closely, it tells the whole story, or at least the one I've been trying to tell. Dorval's play is a secular, a family ritual commemorating fortuitous acts (the father's return) and acts of will (love) that took place in a remembered past. Its characters seek to recover and perpetuate in a representation, assumed like a vestment, a presence that has vanished: their own and their father's, source of covenants of affiliation, moral order, virtue, love. Greek theatre, as Diderot and Rousseau understood it,[62] lives again, the nation shrunk to family size, but the communal and communing spirit still bent back upon itself in congratulatory self-knowledge. How odd that this play, which is taken as an example of a new "realistic" theatre, wedded to historic conditions and manners, should try to situate itself in Eliade's sacred and reversible time, a time "indefinitely repeatable," "an ontological, Parmenidean time" that "neither changes nor is exhausted"![63] Particular, historic details are lovingly tended but at the same time raised by

[62] See the remarkable essays by Lucette Pérol, "Diderot, les tragiques grecs et Brumoy," and Raymond Trousson, "Le Théâtre tragique grec au siècle des lumières," in *Studies on Voltaire and the Eighteenth Century,* 154 (1976), pp. 1593–1616; 155 (1976), pp. 2113–2136.

[63] *The Sacred and the Profane* (New York: Harcourt, Brace & World, 1959), p. 69.

the attitudes of the players and the writer to the status of worshipful symbols. How to account for this tension?

On the very first page of the *Entretiens sur le Fils naturel,* the narrator begins by saying that when he saw the play performed, Lysimond, the father, who was to play his own role, was dead, and so was replaced by one of his friends, a man in physical appearance at least much like Lysimond himself. A pathetic detail. The author and the actors weep, can't go on with the final act. A personal tragedy, of course, but also part of the tragi-comedy of mimesis. At first, when Lysimond was alive, the repetition of an event and the representation of a character was potentially closer than is now possible to being a mirror image of that event and character. But as the distance between *then* and *now* expands, we get, the actors get, some sense of the frailty of quasi-perfect illusionism. Instead of Lysimond, we have Lysimond's look-alike. The performance is one degree further removed from sameness or duplication: it ventures to acknowledge that there are differences, that imitative replacements are necessary. Lysimond's own performance would have been, as it were, an inside job; his friend's will have to be a sympathetic translation, an interpretation of an interpretation. And this takes place in spite of Dorval's efforts to keep time still, to sacralize it and to syncretize its diverse moments. As it turns out, the play, and not merely its performance, suffers from a constant historical erosion. The actors have rewritten their roles: "ici ils adoucirent l'expression, là ils pallièrent un sentiment; ailleurs ils préparèrent un incident" (V, *O.e.,* 86). Constance's declaration of love, the tea scene—all additions and inventions,[64] colorations of a desire not simply to maintain but to explain and decorate the past. The past is twice displaced, first imitated by an original version or gospel, now lost, of the family story, then updated under the pressures of contemporary circumstance and hindsight. To transpose the linguistic categories of Benveniste and Weinrich, "histoire" is polluted by "discours"; commentary increasingly engulfs narration in order, here, to inject or adjust significance. Once inside their own lives, now forced to coil back into the representation of those lives, the characters, like the author, Dorval, are drawn between historically "accurate" detail and the initiatives of inventive, atemporal idealization—the generalized realm of verisimilitude and object lessons. They want the play to tell

[64]The same device, which calls attention to the status of the work as text, historical "chronicle," and revisable manuscript, can be found in *Jacques*. In both instances, Diderot encloses, as Cervantes had, a written space in order to trespass and then flee. The damage to the enclosure (claustrophobic) reveals not only the impossibility of unrelieved absorption or, thematically, of temporal and familial consolidation but the presence, as Thomas M. Kavanagh suggests, speaking of *Jacques*, of "an on-going act of language . . . That which might mask a self-creative act of language has become its mirror" (*The Vacant Mirror: a Study of Mimesis through Diderot's Jacques le fataliste, Studies on Voltaire and the Eighteenth Century,* 104 [Banbury, Oxfordshire: Cheney & Sons, Ltd., 1973], p. 114). Actually, the special quality of Diderot's reflexive works lies in their equivocation: they aspire to be both windows and mirrors, representations and reflections about representing—or, in my terms, insides and self-conscious outsides.

their past, to stabilize the present,[65] but also to form and predict the future: to serve as a metaphor. MOI objects, for example, that the servant Charles speaks to Dorval with too much familiarity: "Cela n'est ni vraisemblable ni vrai" (p. 83). True enough, Dorval replies, for *then* or *now,* but as a child of God Charles deserves to be treated as an equal; in time, there ought to be no servants playing these roles in society or on stage. And even if, in point of fact, Constance never uttered her "déclaration"—or Rosalie her apostrophe: "Amant qui m'étais alors si cher!" (p. 130)—"l'on serait bien à plaindre dans la société, s'il n'y avait acune femme qui lui ressemblât" (p. 85). We might say that profane time, the time of a committed and historic hermeneutic, intersects sacred time to produce in the play new islands of hierophantic moments to rival and displace the old ones that inspired their eruption. Time cannot double back on itself, repeat itself without the help of an historic will that acts as its medium and inevitably interferes as it represents or re-enacts it. Instead of a mirror, a hall once again of temporally deployed and distorting reflections. The risk to the image's identity is part of the purpose.

It may already be clear that the play and its frame (the dialogues surrounding it) are ruled by a system of replace-

[65]Alexander Gelley studies a similar phenomenon in Rousseau's *Nouvelle Héloïse,* concentrating on memory and its "constitutive, sanctifying power," and he accurately, I believe, adduces St. Augustine. His article is called "The Two Julies: Conversion and Imagination in *La Nouvelle Héloïse,*" *MLN,* 92 (May 1977), pp. 753–56. We need a study of Augustinism in the eighteenth century. It seems to me pervasive, as will be apparent in these notes as well as my text.

ments that in one way or another resemble an original model. Charles Collé said more than he intended when he humorously called *Le Fils naturel* "une sodomie théâtrale" in which nothing, including its hero, was "natural." It's not only the case, as Palissot noticed,[66] that the author (Dorval) is also the subject and protagonist of his own play, but that this self-propagation—repetitious overlappings of the same—is echoed and figured in the incestuous or narcissistic relationship of the characters. A single identity or unit, like the homogeneity of sacred time, attempts to sodomize itself and so repeat itself until it has appropriated all difference. It never quite succeeds. Clairville, as Dorval's disciple, splits away from him, amoeba-like, to marry Rosalie, Dorval's sister and secret passion. Likewise, Constance, Rosalie's tutor, reconstructs Rosalie into her own image, only to make of her a perfect wife for her brother. The action of the play, which begins with the unnatural separation of a son from his natural father and sister, and from society itself, threatens *because* of these separations, to end as if by violent reaction in the incestuous exclusion of otherness, the fulfilment of Dorval's passion for his sister, incest itself. But the play skirts this hurdle to draw all the characters into a proto-incestuous bond nonetheless. What is literally defeated is figuratively achieved: the energies of natural cohesiveness, the inbreeding call of Same to Same, brother to sister, father to children, breaks out, legitimized, in a series of Freudian, that is, never fully adequate, substitutions. Should there be

[66]Both Collé and Palissot are cited by Assézat in A-T, VII, 9−10.

an objection that Dorval ends up with nobody like the sister he lost to Clairville, we have to remember that he still broods,[67] but more importantly that Constance, his wife, has come to think and to speak like him—as MOI says to Dorval, "Il y a des expressions, des pensées qui sont moins d'elle que de vous" (p. 125). If not his sister, a partial replica of himself. What makes all these replacements possible is the work of imitation, the fact that, as Constance (sounding like Shaftesbury) puts it: "L'imitation nous est naturelle" (A-T, VII, 67). Where ties of blood are absent, the characters reproduce their own likeness by setting examples for others who can then act as their surrogates. Modern anthropologists would speak of a remarkable "economy" in this society, love relationships patterning themselves over consanguineous ones, and of a perfectly equilibrated "exchange" between the two fraternal, symmetrically arranged couples. No emotion or obligation is lost. Like the style of acting Dorval prescribes, the players destroying an "ordre symétrique" by grouping themselves together, separating, and coming together again (V, *O.e.*, 89), the kinship system is almost balletic in its sinuous continuities.

But in the dissolution of an initial, half-hidden symmetry (Dorval: Rosalie = Clairville: Constance) and the reassembling of a new one (Dorval: Constance = Rosalie: Clairville), though the system remains closed, something yearned for has escaped: the still, singular unity of the self.

[67]For Dorval's chagrin, especially its incestuous implications, see Jacques Chouillet's insightful *La Formation des idées esthétiques de Diderot* (Paris: Armand Colin, 1973), pp. 422–62.

The characters have been adulterated, educated away from what once (we have to suppose) they were. Dorval, whose characteristic attitude is solitary meditation, a flawless insidedness, first moves toward his twin image, Rosalie, and then is forced to relinquish it, replace it. In the end, he only succeeds in scattering and multiplying himself. Rosalie has his blood, Clairville his example, Constance his speech and thought. Together they re-create a dispersed and generalized Dorval that provides them with a common and overlapping ground. And is this not exactly what all of them, including Dorval, try to do with history and their historic past? Identity and sameness, the inside, particular, and sequestered view, now gone, has to be translated, its self-loving impulse still visible, into metaphoric, generalized replacements.

separation, "une teinte obscure"

Dorval appears in the *Introduction,* reappears inside his play; then, with more than one image of himself left behind, he strides out into the second frame, *Dorval et moi,* separate and separated. He's worried over the separation of two families in the neighborhood: "Dorval avait tenté sans succès de terminer une affaire qui divisait depuis longtemps deux familles du voisinage" (p. 80). More sisters and brothers? It seems to be his self-assigned burden to bring about rapprochements or fusions in life and in art, and not to be able to carry them off as he'd like. MOI, the narrator, not I, establishes this link when he notices: "Il en était chagrin, et je vis que la disposition de son âme allait répandre une teinte obscure sur notre entretien." Their "entretien" is of course concerned principally with theatrical illusion, the possibility of drawing art as close as possible to life. But the separations of life preside over the separations of art—or is it the other way around? No matter. Dorval circulating between two families, or Dorval circulating between his play and history or his play and its critic, MOI—the laws are the same. Indeed they are the laws that govern the structural sequence of the *Introduction, Le Fils naturel,* and *Dorval et moi.* First the solitary figure, followed by an event in which he becomes involved, even helps create; then, in the drift of time, from an outside filled with memories, the effort to annex sympathies, to overlap *now* and *then,* family with family, actor and observer. Dorval is the self-chosen instrument of these impossible conciliations. Put yourself in place of this man, he says, this family. Put yourself in my place. Let me explain, interpret, imitate. Give me *all* your attention: "il faut que nous soyons tout entiers à la même chose" (p. 80)—no distracting incidents, secondary actions. Don't stand out there, join me at least imaginatively: "celui qui agit et celui qui regarde, sont deux êtres différents" (p. 81). What isn't now, what never was, may some day be! No "coups de théâtre," nothing to break the continuous, rich melody of sympathy. Does this offend your sense of possibility? I give you my word. Everywhere, Dorval espousing reality, throwing himself bodily over it, joining its separate limbs, asking us to be enchanted with it, with him, to forgive and forget, to become like him (or his characters), an insider. But he hasn't reconciled the neighborhood families, nor has he bedded his sister. His play is not history, its incidents not even "rapprochés de l'expérience journalière" (p. 81); and MOI cannot be sold a bill of goods, even though he saw the play under the best of "intimate" conditions. But the effort is positively extraordinary, in every way exemplary. *Dorval et moi* is hardly an apology for Dorval's play: it forms part of the ongoing attempt (of which the play itself is an illustration) to bend an outside view to the sympathetic understanding of some transacted event (elsewhere: text) or desire. Where there is failure, we're requested not so much to admire his play as to acknowledge the merciless rigors of convention—societal, linguistic, or aesthetic—that keep the artist or the human being from reaching his goal: the re-production of an inside, the duplication of the Same.

Where is Diderot in all of this? Behind but also overlaying MOI. And MOI? Doing the same with Dorval.

Sodomy. And where are *we*? Behind Diderot—that is, fissioning and fusing, in some "unnatural" measure, with them all. (Actually, only solicited.) At one end of this chain, Diderot dallies with us; at the other, Dorval's characters dally with one another. Though it is Diderot's genius that sets out this magnificent diagram, I take it as an unexceptionable truth, one hardly explored, that the author acts with his reader as his characters act with one another. In this instance, as elsewhere in Diderot's work, trying to establish an intimacy in which self-consciousness and separations evaporate. But, as we've seen, this can't occur—and the tension itself works its way into the diagram. At one famous point in the *Entretiens,* Dorval is alone with nature, and silent. MOI is watching him: "Je suivais sur son visage les impressions diverses qu'il en éprouvait; et je commençais à partager son transport, lorsque je m'écriai, presque sans le vouloir: 'Il est sous le charme'" (p. 97). Nature, that object poets used to imitate, seizes Dorval, fills him with its presence as he stands within it. MOI, the reflector, catches the signs rather than the referents and, moved by these, sharing *these,* speaks about the *poet* (not nature) who sparks his reaction.[68] He speaks "presque sans le vouloir." Emotion spreads from object to object and finally, as if releasing itself from a collaborative repetition in kind, voices not itself but the consciousness of

[68]Diderot will make this plain in the *Rêve:* a poet tells his story, and "les instruments sensibles adjacents conçoivent des impressions qui sont bien celles de l'instrument qui résonne, mais non celles, de la chose qui s'est passée" (V, *O.p.,* 368).

its existence out there—in someone who re-presents it best: "Il est sous le charme." MOI's speech breaks the "charme" not only of the poet silently wrapped (rapt) in his object, but of the reflector's bond with the poet and with his own emotion. The emotion is drawn into discourse, the banal recapitulations of consciousness, always slightly off target. It sounds like this: "Il est vrai. C'est ici qu'on voit la nature. Voici le séjour sacré de l'enthousiasme. Un homme a-t-il reçu du génie? il quitte la ville et ses habitants" (p. 97)— Dorval's opening remark, a *prooemium* or a *praecognitio*. Rhetoric replaces "charm." It rehearses and generalizes a memory of feeling, describing how *any* poet comes to feel, the physiology of that feeling, the moment of awareness, the birth of "ideas," not their formal substance. Yet here is the wonder: from the height of this merely discursive rendition, Dorval is reabsorbed into the emotion he describes. As he arrives at the poet's need to "verser au dehors un torrent d'idées qui se pressent, se heurtent et se chassent" (p. 98), speech gives way to the image it paints. Rhetoric suddenly and cyclically flags into silence; the paragraph ends; Dorval and MOI return to their point of departure: "Il se fit entre nous un silence." And the outsiders, MOI and the rest of us, are forever and teasingly barred from the inner life of Nature and the Poet, except as reflectors, except as we react (as Dorval has to his own rhetoric) to signs and metaphors for feeling. The perspectival planes, superimposed, recede from us to the narrator, to MOI, Dorval, and finally Nature. The last opaque image in the text has Nature and the Poet singing each to each, their primal, unarticulated voices mixed—"Qui est-ce qui mêle sa voix au torrent qui tombe de la montagne?"—longing for similitude.

Nature, as Diderot presents her, is forever pregnant, full of her moody truths: "O Nature, tout ce qui est bien est renfermé dans ton sein. Tu es la source féconde de toutes vérités" (p. 98). She has the ontological status for which every reflector and every text yearns: the ability to project herself irresistibly, to double herself, to disburden her likeness within a proximate humanity. Her visibility functions, as we know, like a spell, working its magical fermentations into mind and matter. It may be tautological to say that in spite of this she remains, naturally, herself, unaltered by readers and interpreters, self-perpetuating and self-involved. To be "natural" therefore, every artist, actor, composer, reader, imitating her, has to replay, duplicate this perfect insidedness of feeling or create the illusion of it—find its formal, objective correlative. The musician transcribing Racine's Clytemnestra "fills" himself with her despair, replaces her, then makes her music (pp. 168–69). The actor locates the "accent" of his character as the author studies the "unité de discours" or "ton" of his play (pp. 102–3), the generative subtext over which he composes the necessary gestural or verbal equivalent. From a base of silent desire, of "images terribles" in Clytemnestra's case, or "la violence du sentiment" (p. 102), the artist builds outward toward its metaphoric translation. Just as Dorval and his characters fold back upon an elusive past, so their translations signal, in part, toward an irretrievable, living prose, aiming to be its extension, its gesticulating and visible limb. The *Paradoxe* will make this activity more cerebral and deliberate, but already in *Dorval et moi* the self-sufficient rapture of an imitation about which one hopes to be unable to say that "l'auteur *est sorti de* son sujet" or "l'acteur entraîné *hors de* son rôle" (p. 102; my italics), is challenged. Michael Fried, in his articles about "the principle of self-absorption"[69] in Diderot's aesthetics restates

[69]"Toward a Supreme Fiction: Genre and Beholder in the Art Criticism of Diderot and His Contemporaries," *New Literary History*, 6 (Spring 1975), pp. 543–85, and "Absorption, a Master Theme in Eighteenth-Century French Painting and Criticism," *Eighteenth-Century Studies*, 9 (Winter 1975–76), pp. 139–77. These articles shy away from Diderot's own fictions, ironies, and literary techniques. But to remain strictly at the level of "principle," there seems little doubt that the principle of absorption conforms to the Renaissance concept of a space seen "through a window." Diderot's originality as a theoretician lies in his having emphasized not a separation of viewers and actors but something far more typical of his own literary behavior: a space structurally similar to the space of Baroque art, in which a heightened verisimilitude, among other things, extends fictional space into life. (See Ch. 5, "Space," in John Rupert Martin's recent *Baroque* [New York: Harper & Row, 1977].) His goal was to make us unseen observers and yet to reduce, even more than was possible in the essentially contemplative Baroque, all distance between observers and actors. Deliberately slighting and by-passing the Rococo, though not the Rococo theme of seeing without being seen—a strategy of consciousness which is more than a little erotic—he harnesses the intensities of academic, that is, Baroque action and transfers them to the here and now; other objects, other concerns, divorced from transcendence, draw the absorbed attention of players and viewers—which of course makes all the difference. The modalities, the architecture and semiology of this new space and its objects, the manner in which it acquires meaning, and meaning of what kind, have yet to be studied seriously.

and isolates what Diderot repeatedly and theoretically says himself: "Dans une représentation dramatique, il ne s'agit non plus du spectateur que s'il n'existait pas" (p. 102). This would be true enough if in fact the spectators of *Le Fils naturel* were not, as it happens, on the stage, if Dorval never left it, if MOI (and we) were not so intentionally, though secretly, present in Diderot's mind. If, in other words, the characters in this play could only be seen from behind and had faces and voices only for each other. But what will Fried do with this frame of consciousness, *Dorval et moi*, so hefty that it crushes the "self-absorbed" play and makes of it an occasion for a performance of quite another order? Self-absorption exists here as elsewhere in Diderot's work, in order to be observed, as some kind of ideal though static moment, a pretext or rather pre-text, which has eventually to connect with an outside view. It is a *strategy* for connection, as deliberately menaced as Dorval's desire to have the present and the future reabsorb the past in a changeless time that excludes history and otherness. Yet everything in the play, the characters, the events, indeed the play itself, hovers between being a thing-in-itself, to-itself, and a thing whose importance lies in its present viewing, its explanation and adulteration, its being mediated through a distanced consciousness. Diderot himself is not, finally, the master of a principle of self-absorption, but the philosopher of a problematic of representation, of which self-absorption or self-forgetfullness is only one precarious phase that inevitably leads to a dispersion, a deployment of consciousness. One has to concede, as Dorval did, that the supremely self-absorbed play, if *Le Fils naturel* is an example, has to be performed under extraordinarily intimate conditions, in a "salon," he says, at best before an audience of highly conscious and knowledgeable witnesses or, preferably, before no audience at all. A kind of "happening" in which the actors are backless participants, performers and spectators at the same time. Is Diderot painting himself into a corner? I think not. The play—like Suzanne's soliloquy, ironically and instructively demystified by the *Préface-Annexe*—is rescued from this fate by its examination in *Dorval et moi*, by being assessed as a *cas limite*, and by opening out to larger circles of critical intelligence.

imitative psychology

Let us not forget Diderot's hand traveling to Catherine's thigh, acting as an expelled commentary or supplement to what he's been saying. Can this hand's intention, *before* Catherine's rebuff and therefore before its uneasiness, also serve as a prolegomenon to a theory of sentimentality—and its imminent deconstruction? Diderot's hand looks to be as generous in its impulse as Dorval's gift of Rosalie, his blood and limb, to Clairville, of his dramatic theories to MOI and us, or of his replica of the past (the play) to the present and the future. Generosity, we'd say, but one that tinkers and cajoles: it conveys something but pleads for a return, if only the pleasure of leaving its mark (or bruise) on the merchandise or the recipient. MOI, after commending Dorval's "générosité," scolds him for tormenting Clairville uselessly, much the way Hardouin's "victims," about twenty years later, reproach Hardouin. "Après un violent effort," Dorval answers, "il est une sorte de délassement auquel il est impossible de se refuser, et que vous connaîtriez si l'exercice de la vertu vous avait été pénible. Vous n'avez jamais eu besoin de respirer . . . Je jouissais de ma victoire. Je faisais sortir du coeur de mon ami les sentiments les plus honnêtes; je le voyais toujours plus digne de ce que je venais de faire pour lui. Et cette action ne vous paraît pas naturelle!" (p. 129). An effort—and its recompense: the imperious need to tamper or to touch, in one or the other sense, actually a supplement to the original effort, its shadow, or better, its x-rayed structure. Sentimentality is this movement toward possession *through* generosity, a generosity that wants to disburse itself in order to marshal and control its objects: the things or feelings bestowed and the people upon whom they're bestowed.[70] Its model is economic: the miser or the speculator, an overtly benign though covertly rapacious capitalism. Or its model is racial—as one might expect from the word "générosité" in its classical sense—a measured distribution of blood that assures a multiplication of the flock, a progeny stabilized by the ancestral image and its cautious investment. No wonder then that sentimental litterature is rife with *cris du sang, préjugés nobiliaires,* and with questions of wealth and legacy. It has to postulate, within itself or between itself and its public, a paratactic order, either in the beginning or as an incipient possibility, the dispersion of some original unit or unity, family and family members, speaker and listener, self and world, the scattering of tongues, knowledge,[71] and

---

[70]Prévost, speaking of Nivelle de la Chaussée, in the 1730's, already noticed that "tout Ecrivain qui sait comme lui *réunir* le coeur par le ressort de la tendresse et de la *générosité* est toujours sûr de plaire" (my italics; cited in Marie-Rose de Labriolle, *Le "Pour et contre" et son temps, Studies on Voltaire and the Eighteenth Century,* 34 [Geneva: Institut et Musée Voltaire, 1965], 244).

[71]The *Encyclopédie* can be viewed in this perspective, not only as B. Groethuysen has, as the product of the need to hoard (one can discount, I think, his theory that this is an exclusively bourgeois privilege), but as a sentimental product, advertising the need for a fixed currency. Describing his desire for a steady language of science and philosophy, Diderot foresees the possibility of overcoming all spatial and temporal dislocations in a communal unity of understanding: "Supposé cet idiome admis & fixé, aussitôt les notions deviennent permanentes; la distance des temps disparaît; les lieux se touchent; il se forme des

consciousness itself. Its language tries to *overcome* ellipsis—
Diderot was reproached for this, his stammering *points de
suspension*—expressions that flag on the point of syntactic
juncture or enunciation, the referent unspeakable or
ineffably distanced from its linguistic sign. Action, linguistic, moral, or spiritual, comes as the damnable, adventitious,
unfortunate break in an otherwise continuous, smoothly
functioning whole. The battleground of sentimentality
therefore is change, its divinity Fortune, a life in time,
which, from Regnard's *Le Joueur* to Moore's *The Gamester,*
figures as an unsettling gamble with chance, the attempt to
harness and outwit it, to make it serve rather than destroy.
The roots of sentimentality reach back to the shifting
economic, political, and social soil of the early century, but
also to a new concept of culture in time rather than by
indefinitely fixed values, a culture titillated by "mouvement" and "curiosité," aesthetic as well as intellectual: "les
différentes vues de l'esprit sont presque infinies et la
nature l'est véritablement."[72] Fontenelle's nice irony, its
adventurous optimism allowing for pluralism and difference, inaugurates or rather corresponds to the slow
erosion of classical stasis and the eccentric (often far more
feverish) disorder we associate with rococo art, aesthetics,
and literature. To all of this, sentimentality offers a solution

---

liaisons entre tous les points habités de l'espace & de la durée, & tous les
êtres vivants & pensants s'entretiennent" (ENCYCLOPEDIE, H, VII,
189).

[72]*Préface sur l'utilité des mathématiques et de la physique, et sur les travaux
de l'académie des sciences* (1733) in *Oeuvres* (Paris: Jean-Francois Bastien,
1790), VI, 70.

or at any rate an imaginative counterideal: the gathering-in and fusion of disparate parts and views, a stilling of time, consciousness, identity, speech, the tearful joy of reunion.[73] Beverley's apartment, as Diderot's *Le Joueur* opens, is a symbolic shambles, "le spectacle du désordre" (H, XI, 341), his fortune scattered, his servants, even the faithful Jarvis, dismissed, his wife, son, sister, pining. Disruption occurs in *Le Philosophe sans le savoir* when Vanderk fils risks the snug intimacy of family life to challenge an illusory enemy to a duel. The atmosphere of the household, the theme of the play, is mercantile prudence and storage, Vanderk the "philosopher" accumulating property relentlessly, warning his servant (bookkeeper) to shut the door from the inside, putting his money into "caisses," "hottes," "magasins fermés," and packing his human cargo, friends and enemies alike, into his salon or his family. The "commerçant" as "l'homme de l'univers" (Act II, sc. 4), a monarch who dispenses liberality, a "rivière de diamants," in order to

[73]This definition of sentimentality is intended to cover only the eighteenth-century phenomenon in its historic context. The term is today overdetermined, but nor for that entirely inapplicable. R. F. Brissenden, whose definition is not exactly mine, intelligently extends its usage to describe nineteenth- and twentieth-century works; but Alan Wilde most perceptively and illuminatingly sets it dialectically against different forms of irony, with the result that the ever-changing content and style of sentimentality is specified by its historic countervision and counterstyle. Precisely because the term has become flabby and pejorative, Wilde proposes, for the twentieth century, the term "anironic," first in "Desire and Consciousness: The 'Anironic' Forster," *Novel*, 9 (Winter 1976) and then, even more broadly, in "Modernism and the Aesthetics of Crisis," *Contemporary Literature*, 20 (Winter 1979).

grow richer, smother dissent, domesticate and unite the realm. Even in so slight a sketch as *Les Pères malheureux*—not to go on with the list—we're offered, as the curtain rises, the spectacle of two desolate huts framed on either side by steep, forbidding mountains, "l'horreur d'un beau paysage," sublime because awesome, awesome because distant, symbols of a fearful rift between the old Simon and the family he loves, and then, as we discover, between father and son, parents and children, past and present, wealth and poverty, private property and humane feeling, law and instinctive need. In all these works, as in *Le Fils naturel,* there is a climactic remelting of severed pairs, pent-up secrets—sometimes trivial, playful, and deliberately contrived—exploding and settling back into silence, differences and distances overcome in sudden ejaculations of intimacy and generosity. The double image realigns itself into one, or at least that realignment is sensed as a possibility, even when it isn't realized.

But are we dealing with moral psychology when we speak of sentimentality, or with mimesis? Is it Dorval's benevolence or his play and his meditations on art that we invoke, speaking of a thwarted desire for fusion and appropriation, the need to imitate and be imitated, to translate and mediate experience? Confluence or interference? One can't be sure. Dorval's characters are, like him, artists, who delineate or play themselves while psychologically they imitate each other, aiming at a unified articulation of the group. Mimesis consumes psychology, perpetuates itself through these people, its energies as masterful and productive as invested capital. To find a double is to double the fund, to extend oneself without risk. But this is precisely the function of *sensibilité*, historically united, together with "realism," to sentimentality. A strange alliance perhaps, but each member, in this necessary confusion of modes of feeling and literary strategies, part of the same design: to unite consciousness with its object so that there is no remainder, nothing in what the object signals that isn't re-produced even to its most physical and wordless effects. "Poète," asks Diderot, using his favorite musical and Platonic analogy, "êtes-vous sensible et délicat? Pincez cette corde; et vous l'entendrez résonner, ou frémir dans toutes les âmes."[74] *Sensibilité* doubles itself without obstruction, and realism, which envies *sensibilité's* easy production of similitude, tries to duplicate the audience and its milieu in the work and to transform every physical surface into a resounding signifier. Instead of reverberating strings, sympathetic mirrors. Realism takes silent possession of the physical world in order to turn it to account—by which I mean, to multiply its likeness and its semiological effects. As Marmontel put it, commenting on theorists of sentimentality: "S'il fallait en croire quelques spéculateurs modernes, tout dans les arts devrait concourir à ce qu'ils appellent l'*effet,* c'est-à-dire à l'illusion et à l'émotion la plus forte."[75] Realism is the conscious, the outside striving for effects that *sensibilité* transmits automatically from within. Both, as I've said, strategies of signs, since the shudder of sentimentality comes on as we're

[74]*De la poésie dramatique,* A-T, VII, 195.
[75]*Eléments de littérature,* II, 488.

transported to what this currency, these gestures and actions or those props, implies: the gold bullion, as it were, buried in the minds and hearts of characters and audience alike. These signs write their checks over, and so imitate, a universal treasury of *droiture, probité, vertu, raison,* "sentiments de la nature et de la reconnaissance" (Vanderk), etc., guarantors once again of social unity, coherence, and perpetuity. The psychology of imitation is also then a psychology of reference and allusion, aiming at the resurrection or the revaluation of signifiers. Its "generosity" extends, in this sense, to the recuperation of lost or threatened meanings, for which it provides metaphoric signs, fictional equivalents. Dorval, sentimentally re-writing the past, his characters re-enacting it, recover not classical "règles," but "le fondement de la règle" (V, *O.e.,* 82), imitative desire itself, the treasure house of instinctive recovery and mimetic communality. Viewed diachronically rather than synchronically, sentimentality and its friends *sensibilité* and realism are therefore forms of primitivism, attempts to reach and then to translate some original experience of world, self, or text, to provide a gestural, physical, or linguistic trace of these. Neo-Classicism rises therefore as naturally out of sentimental mimesis as David rises out of Greuze.

Imitative psychology tries to gratify itself, that is, reproduce itself instantaneously. Its rhetoric wants to be persuasive with a vengeance, as automatic in its effect as a twitch, a tear, or a grimace, a sign for a sign. Nothing, it *pretends,* is mediated by reflection or by art. Nature speaks; we imitate and are imitated. Imitation is the instructive purpose of sentimental works, the production of an outside that reflects the inside. Homogenization. This is no longer "exemplary" literature; it aspires to be exactly duplicative in technique and result. Diderot's vulgarization in *Le Fils naturel* and its dialogues, at the height of his sentimentality—my reason for considering it at length and as a final example, though each of us will find his or her own—culminates in this recognizable paradox of imitative desire: it can only instruct or transmit instruction by positing its presence, its own hand—on Catherine's knee, or in its personal, artful, and manipulative interventions. It has to let go and allow itself the sight of its own deconstruction, the afterglow of consciousness and conscience. The winds of Romantic irony are already blowing, not gustily, but with alternating drafts of remorse and pleasure. It is as if Diderot had to burrow down inside things, take the urge to its limit, the urge to pry, connect, and relate, had to offer this lesson, indeed this new sensibility, before he could feel these winds that drive around countless paradoxes. Instruction can (cannot) be automatic, art can (cannot) be nature, and (nor) time stilled; imitation is (is not) generous and ever (never) duplicative; *sensibilité* imprisons as much as it excites compliance; it is instinctive and organic or imitatively self-induced and self-advertising; a translation is (never) a true replacement; the paired oppositions that sentimentality hopes to refocus, reawaken outside the work; language has endlessly to supplement the tedium of silence and gesture, to speak for or about them.

The regrettably loose or menacingly constrictive knot of absorption, of unified mood and sentimental sympathy, within Diderot's fiction of the 60's and 70's is increasingly undone, morally and aesthetically. The alternating rhythm of narration and intrusive (actually extrusive) commentary quickens; consciousness (the author's, or the narrator's, or the characters') is itself thematized, separated from its fictional constructions, often divided between itself and its witness. At the same time, the subject matter of these works is invariably concerned, as earlier, with the possibility of unity of one kind or another, "unité de caractère," the microscopic continuity of matter, unity of "action" or theatrical performance, familial, social, or legal solidarity, fidelity in love. And in each case, the ambiguously desired cohesiveness, simultaneity, or suspension, held in place by momentary desire, natural forces, attention, will, imitative vibration—and for the mediator-writer, by his fabulation —threatens to or does in fact explode, like the oak tree and our own bodies in *Le Rêve*, "en cent mille éclats" (V, *O.p.*, 260), pieces of matter or desire, separate organs or "brins," a random splatter of minutes and spaces, divided lovers, selves, and opinions, a "stochastic cloud," to use Jeffrey Mehlman's term,[76] of anarchic energies. The themes of these works describe or their action in time and space proceed through moments of aggregation and disintegration,

[76]"Cataract: Diderot's Discursive Politics, 1749–1751," *Glyph 2* (Baltimore: The Johns Hopkins Press, 1977), p. 40.

union and disjunction—Suzanne, to use her melodramatic example, listening to Mme de Moni ("on s'unissait à elle; l'âme tressaillait, et l'on partageait ses transports" [B, *O.r.*, 259]); Suzanne in a sexual heat of communication ("je l'interrompais, ou je la devançais, ou je parlais avec elle" [p. 282]); and between these incidents, Suzanne enduring spiritual and physical alienation ("je fus renfermée dans ma cellule; on m'imposa le silence; je fus séparée de tout le monde, abandonnée à moi-même" [p. 243]). The enormous attraction for Diderot of the picaresque structure of *Jacques,* where life is lived and spoken amidst a willed or accidental eruption of events and imitations, scenes of social and sentimental in-gathering, concentration, and secrecy, followed by scenes of dilation and dispersal, lies in the portrayal of the mind's and life's own unstemmable "evaporation" and divagation. When M. Renardeau notices, in *La Pièce et le prologue,* written probably within the span of *Jacques'* composition, that Hardouin is distracted, Hardouin-Diderot replies: "Mon ami, je suis excédé de ce mauvais pays-ci. La vie s'y évapore. On n'y fait quoi que ce soit."[77] But Hardouin "evaporates," allows himself to be deflected from a steady literary course, with a vigor and joy he can't conceal. The constrictions of ambition and conscience are not less troublesome than the walls of Paris or life, and within both, deviant and strategically liberating *écarts* or arrangements that temporarily confuse expectation, his

[77] In my edition of *Est-il bon? Est-il méchant?*, *Studies on Voltaire and the Eighteenth Century,* 16 (Geneva: Institut et Musée Voltaire, 1961), 222.

own and others', are possible. Dissolution is viewed as a fact of life, welcomed as a relief, bemoaned as a loss.

The cloud of reflective consciousness that gathers round and inside these works, even inside a play like *Est-il bon? Est-il méchant?*,[78] does not dissolve however, even though parts of it vaporize irresistibly into the different densities of comment and imitation. If the strangely insistent meteorological indications of *Le Supplément* and *Mme de la Carlière* represent a "stochastic" fog, from which the action, events, and characters are precipitated, the authorial consciousness in both is not so much this fog as the clouds, "ces énormes ballons qui nagent ou restent suspendus dans l'atmosphère," and which "demeurent là comme des morceaux de sucre au fond d'une tasse de café qui n'en saurait plus prendre."[79] It would in fact be far better to speak of layers of clouds, clouds of various altitude, the lower ones alternately represented by the ironic and mordant Countess, Mme de la Carlière's cousin, and the

[78]Though plays are not supposed to have both these densities, that is, no "point of view" since according to Robert Scholes, "no one stands between the audience and the action" (*Elements of Fiction* [New York: Oxford University Press, 1968], p. 26), Diderot manages even in a theatrical work to contrive a "comment." In *La Pièce* and *Est-il bon? Est-il méchant?*, where the action is itself an embedded play, we can establish a point of view (on the action) in Hardouin, another, more dispersed, in Hardouin's victims as they judge his and their "performance," and a third, Diderot's own, which shapes and so judges its autobiographical material.

[79]Citations from Diderot's *Contes* are taken from Herbert Dieckmann's edition (London: University of London Press, 1963). The present reference is to p. 153.

narrator's interlocutor. Dorval may have, as an after-thought, toyed with the idea of parodying his play, but these two instantaneously either suppress their guffaws or impudently ridicule the story's most sentimental moment: Mme de la Carlière's speech to her small circle of relatives and friends, when "l'honnête réunit leur suffrages, les confond, les rend uns," and when these friends together create "ce bonheur qui nous assimilait" (p. 160). The cirrus clouds that stretch above them have a steadier moral course and extend into the *Supplément,* where they disclose their meaning. And whereas there may be a certain entropic "degradation of energy" within the action of these fictions, as Mehlman says, as far as the bodies, hopes, and desires of some of the characters are concerned, there is no abatement of the energies of consciousness and mimesis.[80] It is merely the forms and levels of consciousness that change (and conflict and influence one another) as they do within Mme de la Carlière's circle and "le public," in those

---

[80]"Cataract," pp. 52–53. Mehlman's water sports are fascinating and obviously inviting, but I must confess they are bewildering. He does not make sufficient distinctions between "vapors," "fogs," and "clouds," though he does seem to be suggesting an "irreducibility of vapor out of which the action of the *conte [Madame de la Carlière]* emerges" (p. 53). Is this the "activity of narration (*récit*)" or of "the events narrated (*histoire*)" (p. 52)? And where does the implied author, as distinct from the narrator, stand in this watery chaos? We may after all be in full agreement, when the fog lifts. The "decline of physical and moral energy" in Diderot's characters, and in the *histoire,* may illustrate the second law of thermodynamics, but what will not, in Western fiction from Homer to Beckett? Mehlman does better with Lucretius.

nether or upper regions where discourse, the image of life, is refracted and reinterpreted.

Both Diderot and Diderot's fiction in these years make consciousness and its inventions a matter of the tensile and wavering "tone" ("un ton variable") of perception. Consciousness in the *Rêve* is no longer the mechanical figurine of the *Lettre sur les sourds*, mounted on the chiming bell of a clock, grimacing at discordant sounds, smiling on harmony, passively attentive, as in Locke and Hume, to the assault of sensations. In the *Rêve*, the celebrated "origine du faisceau," which is only part of a "system" of perception, is not soldered onto the body, but "emanates" from the soft, insensate substance that serves as its pillow and that structures itself into the entire living organism: "il émane d'une substance molle, insensible, inerte qui lui sert d'oreiller" (V, *O.p.*, 331). It may "dilate" or "condense" the limits of perception, perception of the world and of one's body-in-the-world (p. 333); it may surrender to or countermand the independent percepts of one or another physical organ. But except in the case of the truly mad, "les imbéciles" (p. 354), it remains in a state of dialectic tension. One cannot here speak of consciousness as a steady state, but as a sequence of body-mind phases that alternately tangle and unscramble illusion, reality, and desire. The fact that Mlle de L'Espinasse, while dreaming, can feel her "body-image"[81]

[81]The now considerable corpus of literature on "body-image" or "body boundary" (see the work of Seymour F. Fisher, Sidney E. Cleveland, Seymour Wapner, and Heinz Werner) fails to mention Diderot as a forerunner. These psychological studies open up new areas for aesthetics, but only a group of Yale architects has profited from

swell to dimensions greater than Ovid's sea-goddess at the moment of creation (p. 334) or that d'Alembert is himself also this kind of haptic dreamer, tells us that a certain style of poesis is simply the successful record of one such phase. Eventually, consciousness oscillates out of its representations. Any long-sustained performance by any portion of the perceptual system falls under suspicion as unnatural, self-destructive, immoral, or fanatical. The heaving

---

them, as far as I can tell (see Kent C. Bloomer and Charles W. Moore, *Body, Memory, and Architecture* [New Haven: Yale University Press, 1977], especially Ch. 5). In an informative book called *Self: An Introduction to Philosophical Psychology* (New York: Pegasus, 1969), Gerald E. Myers provides a summary of the relationship of self, imagination, and body fantasy (Ch. 7) that might be harnessed for literary theory. A greater sense of "boundary definiteness" causes, it appears, greater communicativeness, independence, and motivation—in my terms, a greater awareness of "outsides" (readers) and of being "outside" of oneself; less "boundary definiteness," the reverse, and again in my terms, an increased centripetal energy, absorption in the self, or in the "inside" activity of mimesis. Further: "Whereas the definite-boundaried person tends to experience his bodily sensations in the skin and muscles, the indefinite-boundaried individual tends to feel them interiorly, *in the heart and stomach*" (p. 109; my italics). The similarity to Diderot's polarity of the "sage" and the "homme sensible" is stunning, and one wonders whether people in general or only geniuses like Diderot are not able to upset or manipulate these boundaries. My later discussion of narrative distance and vulnerability seems, in this perspective, to pinpoint precisely the social as well as the literary consequences of bodyboundaries. Here is Myers on the psychological issue: "People vary in how *vulnerable* they feel their bodies to be. [Substitute "voices" or "texts" for "bodies."] Some may feel their bodily surfaces to be soft, porous, even vulnerable to penetration by space itself; whereas others enjoy [or invent] a body-image that is hard and resilient at the boundaries" (p. 109).

123

"diaphragm" of *sensibilité,* the tiny "point" toward which "l'origine du faisceau" may concentrate its activity, the absorption of imitation, all diminish the full scope of consciousness, create in Diderot a dread, which spells itself out in his later work, of being trapped, victimized, embarrassed, or reduced. Actors, in or out of *Le Paradoxe,* on or off stage, become particularly interesting to Diderot in this sense too, since they walk the narrow line between conscious creation and absorption, forcing themselves and their audiences to withdraw from the real world to the script of one—an exercise of power which may also be the willful or automatic short-circuiting of their and our consciousness. Hardouin's friends, who were compelled to perform the roles he assigned them, revile him because his scenario and his acting have been too convincing: "Plus, plus de confiance en celui qui peut feindre avec tant de vérité" (p. 395). Readers may censure Mme de la Pommeraye, saying, "Je ne me fais pas à un ressentiment d'une si longue tenue; à un tissu de fourberies, de mensonges, qui dure près d'un an." The narrator agrees: "Ni moi non plus, ni Jacques, ni son maître, ni l'hôtesse" (B, *O.r.,* 652). Resentment springs from the *duration* as well as the stiff mastery of the art of funneling consciousness, whose ultimate concern is freedom and whose ultimate dread is being pressured from within or made subservient to its own or someone else's imitation. We have not sufficiently reckoned with the fact that fatalism in *Jacques* is actually the belief or fantasy that we are inside and enacting a universal scenario, "*écrit* là-haut." Jacques and his master live with the possibility that they travel and speak within a constraining discourse and that their only freedom is the alteration of that language, the ability to reformulate, reiterate, and translate the already spoken.[82] Diderot's last fiction is the trial of the consciousness of fiction, on many levels, its author pushing ever outward to encircle (unlike Rousseau, whom we shall see pushing inward to be encircled in) the consciousness of life as consciousness of the belief in the mimetic design or "action" of life—and this, in spite of the alternating dispersals and consolidations within his own consciousness.

How unique is Diderot in his ascent? Hegel, who uses Diderot's Rameau to forward his argument about the advent of an Absolute Spirit or pure consciousness, is himself the ramification of a movement not entirely peculiar to the eighteenth century, but at no previous time more pervasive. My purpose in raising the mortifying

[82]Thomas M. Kavanagh intelligently insists, in *The Vacant Mirror,* on the reflexive nature of *Jacques,* on the primacy of the *énonciation* and *le temps de l'écriture,* which put "reality" or the mimetic function of (all) narrative in question. Diderot's "actualization of a limited number of narrational alternatives" (p. 11) has, even if we take Kavanagh's suggestion and dwell within the prison-house of language, a mimetic function: the self-conscious or parodic imitation of mimetic language; and the "outside and pre-existing" sequence would, in the case of *Jacques,* be not the temporal, empirical world but the narrative time of the language of "le grand rouleau," another "act of language which," according to Kavanagh, speaking more generally, "rules all" (p. 53). Critics who, in their "mimetic analysis," deprive language of its "self-sufficiency" and who, in so doing, resurrect a "pre-existing 'real' as banal as it is mythic" (p. 75), may be allowed, I think, to contemplate, as Diderot did, the banal, mythic, but troublesome reality of a predetermined discourse *about* reality.

question is numbly to suggest the complexity of and the need for a history of distancing consciousness (of the decidedly impure kind) as it is reflected in the "progress" of literary forms. Such a history would eventually have to encompass the ideologies and styles of relationship in social and political life, the distance between subjects and their objects in epistemology and religion, and correlate these with one another and with the "frames" and distances one finds in literary works. (At the end of the nineteenth and in the early twentieth century, the spatial categories of this history, ardently deliberated and lived in Romanticism and the preceding century, become the explicit, normative, and axial features of *Einfühlung* psychology and aesthetic theory from Lotze to Lipps, from Worringer to Vernon Lee, Brecht, Bullough, and Joseph Frank.) The space of language models itself upon and also against the preconceptions and power strategies of a social and metaphysical space, imaginatively reshaping boundaries and the possibilities of human exchange. It responds, according to Jean Duvignaud, to "the expectations and demands revealed by men during periods of change, because it acts as a mirror or a schema of a freedom which seeks through (or in spite of) old determinisms to suggest new relationships between men."[83] With this in mind, at least some features of a history

[83]*The Sociology of Art,* tr. T. Wilson (New York: Harper and Row, 1972), pp. 89–90. It is interesting to note that a new group of sociologists and historians are turning toward a phenomenological "cognitive aesthetics" in order to overcome the epistemological crisis in their fields, turning, that is, toward the recovery of "the Renaissance notion that the human world is constituted by acts of human intelligence, imagination,

of literary consciousness seem relatively clear, if consciousness is located and exemplified, somewhat restrictively, as a start, in the distance between the teller and the told, the distance created by narrative "frames," defined by Uspensky as "a shift between the internal and external authorial positions."[84]

The forms of power, relationship, and freedom this consciousness stabilizes is, as I've proposed, a reflection of those same forms operating among characters and ideologies in the work. Beginning then with the strict enforcement of narrative distance in Classicism, a "frame," as in *La Princesse de Clèves*, which absorbs the atomistic individualism or egocentricity of the characters, their fear of *enlisement*, of sinking gullibly into the illusions of secular life, of losing Stoic, Epicurean, or Augustinian vigilance or "repose," we might draw a graph of this distance through the eighteenth

---

and will." In *Structure, Consciousness, and History*, eds. R. H. Brown and S. M. Lyman (Cambridge: Cambridge University Press, 1978), articles by Louis Marin and Rom Harré touch on the area of literary discourse and its relationship to social forms. Harré's statement, not developed in his article "Architectonic man: On the structuring of lived experience," is reminiscent of Duvignaud and worth quoting at length, especially for the citation from Coleridge: "I wish to stress even more strongly the existent character of social forms but also to emphasize that those forms only 'fluoresce in the light of a rhetoric,' as Coleridge put it. This allows the student of the sociology of knowledge to turn his attention to the principles of the transformational processes by which icons in thought are realized as structures in the *Umwelt* and to examine the forms of the latter in terms of shifting rhetorics" (p. 143).

[84]*A Poetics of Composition*, tr. V. Zavarin and S. Wittig (Berkeley and Los Angeles: University of California Press, 1973), p. 151.

century, the line hesitantly bifurcating, one segment swerving toward imitative sympathy, the "internal position," the other steady in its course or mounting reactively to the descent of the first. Where the two positions are maintained in a single author—and this occurs in the greatest of them—the way is prepared for those antinomies of distance characteristic of Romanticism. In this bird's eye view, the most extraordinary display of equivocal distance is to be found in Marivaux, though one could adduce other figures of the early century—Crébillon *fils,* Prévost, Voltaire, or Montesquieu, whose narrators are confronted with "insides," at times their own, about which they or the authors draw frames that block or complicate their relationship with what is described. The barely visible frame an author sets around an obtuse narrator, the dead space between letters in an epistolary novel, the frames one character builds around another or about himself, the use of an eccentric or exotic rhetoric are all occasions for ironic disjunction. In *Les Liaisons dangereuses,* in many ways the climactic fulfillment of these fictions, it is not so much the acclaimed multiplication of "points of view" that scores the ironic and ideological point, as the (useless) effort to unframe the self and frame every other, to maintain a state of transcendent "backlessness,"[85] the speakers hidden or

[85] I owe this term to Lionel Gossman, whose conversation, like Diderot's, is a cascade of marvels. He used it to describe Voltaire. The metaphor is perfect, since it combines a "body-image" (see n. 81 above) and a literary device. The backless writer lets us see only his reason and vigilance and makes us feel naked. He is, paradoxically, the opposite of what we mean when we say, colloquially, "up front," so that our tempta-

entirely dissolved (Mme de Merteuil) behind their perfected disguise or their armor of "reason." In these authors the very principle of imitation is suspect: to fall within the area bordered by a frame, to be marked as "author" or "character" (Héros or Héroïne de roman, Prude, Céladon, Dévote, Amant, Prêcheuse, Nouvelle Dalila, or for that matter, though later, Nouvelle Héloïse), is to descend into the repetitious, often sordid and violent, fictions of desire, social code, or of fiction itself. They have learned, we might say, not only from Saint-Sorlin's visionaries or Molière's Cathos and Magdelon that "le tissu de notre roman"—our imaginary, copied projects—ridiculously outwits the possibilities of our condition, but also, from Mme de La Fayette and Augustinian Classicism generally, that life and history foolishly but inevitably, like original sin, imitate themselves through our imitations of *them*.[86] A language

---

tion is to find his vulnerable front *behind* him. Few critics of Voltaire, even today, have been bold enough to look. In the case of Mme de Merteuil, whose every letter is a strategy, we can never locate a self: the last in a long line of masked figures, her mask has become flesh. The same can be said of the way the novel is framed: there is no telling the manipulative power of the frame from the manipulation inside the work, with the result that the reader-critic is himself framed: "In observing the process whereby the novel continues to include outside observers within itself, the critic of critics cannot, without repeating the critical error he set out to expose, claim immunity for himself" (Irving Wolfarth, "The Irony of criticism and the criticism of irony: a study of Laclos criticism," *Studies on Voltaire and the Eighteenth Century*, 48 (1974), 271).

[86] The fact that I locate the ideology of repetition or imitation within a Christian context will no doubt mortify anti-Robertsonians who instinctively recoil at the sign of the cross. The recent work of René

that evokes our condition, that has its ancient, magical privilege—as it does only most energetically in Racine—of creating presence, recrystallizes that condition and contagiously perpetuates it. (The Princesse de Clèves falls into history and society not directly by involving herself with the court, but by being insistently "prepared" for it, fed and so poisoned with imitations, *récits* told *about* life's—the court's—irresistible reduplication of behavior.)

If the early Enlightenment seems bent on improvement, that improvement announces itself in its narratives as a dream of consciousness severed from its own testimony and captured helplessly in its frames. And surrounded by these frames, sex, masks, words, all social and political inevitabilities perform their wanton imitations and repetitions. Usbek must return to his body and his harem; Meilcour, whose training shows in the cynical "thèses générales,"[87] epithets, and maxims, the aesthetic cover he's learned from those around him is more "éclairé"

Girard and of W. Pierre Jacoebée argues implicitly in favor of such an interpretation. Though Jacoebée's *La Persuasion de la Charité: Thèmes, formes et structures dans les Journaux et Oeuvres diverses de Marivaux* (Amsterdam: Rodopi, 1976) is not concerned with repetitions or imitation in the sense I've been using, he carefully scores the point that the origins of *sensibilité* lie in the Christian writings of French Classicism and that this early version of it inspires the theme of behavioral deviance and the fact of mimetic deviance in Marivaux—to whom I will be turning shortly. For Jacoebée, "une marche d'emprunt," an imitated discourse or gesture, follows a sinful order or "principe d'orgueil" and so estranges us from the order of charity and natural particularity (p. 131).

[87]Claude Crébillon, *Les Egarements du coeur et de l'esprit,* ed. Etiemble (Paris: Armand Colin, 1961), p. 106.

because more "corrompu" (p. 211); Des Grieux, who moons over the fourth book of the *Aeneid,* as Prévost did, can't help but repeat its tragedy. These figures and others relive the *peregrinatio* topos, typically wandering physically or morally back to an inalterable social place or condition, and no consciousness or frame of reference saves them. In all cases, as Jean Roudaut says, speaking of early eighteenth-century poets: "Ils ne tentent pas d'adapter leur langage au monde, mais de soumettre le monde à leur système mental"[88] —that is, to their special poetics of reason (Usbek), wit (Meilcour), and tenderness (Des Grieux). These systems merely hoist a divorced and impotent authorial consciousness onto a scaffold from which, like Voltaire writing his stories or his life of Charles XII, it can shape the repetitive mess of history into tragedy,[89] or into ironic symmetries and cycles.

[88]*Poètes et grammariens au XVIIIe siècle* (Paris: Gallimard, 1971), p. 36. Roudaut indicates how this language, which constitutes the poet's mental and "speaking" being, distances him from the world: "S'enfermant dans le langage, la poésie est devenue une description *à distance* du monde."

[89]See Lionel Gossman, "Voltaire's Charles XII: History into Art," *Studies on Voltaire and the Eighteenth Century,* 25 (1963) and *French Society and Culture: Background for Eighteenth-Century Literature* (Englewood Cliffs, N.J.: Prentice-Hall, 1972). If I do not discuss Voltaire at length, it is because Gossman's studies, as they focus on Voltaire, explain my position eloquently: "Literature, for Voltaire, is a kind of cosmetic, skillfully working over and building its own system out of an irrational and basically unintelligible material which it can never overcome and on which in the last resort it is dependent." I would only add that Voltaire's "material" is often textual rather than phenomenal and that the choice

In Marivaux too, forms of feeling and intelligence hover between natural and acquired, unconscious and conscious modes of imitation. Repetition is his earliest, most pervasive theme; traditions of fiction serve as metaphors for the vortices of fate. *Les Aventures de *** ou les Effets surprenants de la sympathie, La Voiture embourbée,* and *Pharsamon ou les Folies romanesques* ironically conform to established narrative codes and within these codes fasten not only on familiar typologies (set characters, borrowed incidents and even narrative voices) but especially on the structuring principles of repetition and return in order to exorcise, reflexively and through parody, the very concept of pre-emptive design and influence—or what underlies it: "sympathie" for that design or influence. Narrators and characters crave the release of "chance" and "uniqueness," of a particularity that would break rules or "thèses générales," the mirrors of ordinary practice or ideology. When we speak of mirrors in Marivaux, we are really concerned with horoscopic objects, real mirrors of course, but also books and other people, that cause a startling confusion of insides

---

of these texts—from Biblical lore to Byzantine romance—depends also on their "irrational" qualities, artistic analogues of the phenomenal, which he parodies, must parody perhaps, because they come perilously close to thrilling him. The question of distance in Voltaire's *contes,* briefly touched upon in Henri Coulet's "La distanciation dans le roman et le conte philosophique" (*Roman et lumières au dix-huitième siècle* [Paris: Editions Sociales, 1970], p. 442), is more complex than usually acknowledged. Coulet, who has with remarkable perception read more novels than health ordinarily allows, limits himself to distance as a break in illusion.

and outsides, his characters stalking their doubles with the "curiosité fatale"[90] of erotic gamesters in *Le Bilboquet,* seduced by resemblance into indentity, walking *through* the looking glass into the petrifying myth of their psychological and social selves. Since these mirrors act as frames for consciousness, one can easily understand the resistance at the surface of the glass. The transit from "he," "she," or "they" to "I" corresponds precisely to the distance not only of characters from their predictable human vanities, but of Marivaux and his narrators from the mirrors of conventional fiction and from any subject matter. All of this, including the equation between characters and narrators, Marivaux himself makes plain in the very first "Feuille" of the *Spectateur français,* an author's "apology," containing two typical narratives causally linked to it. In one of these the narrator tells us that he owes his vocation as a journalist not to Addison and Steele, as we might expect, but to his love for a girl whom he took to be innocent and without guile, "belle sans y prendre garde,"[91] until he spied her at the mirror, striking poses she'd used on him.[92] The incident is postponed to the end of the article, but as in Montaigne's essays, it may be taken as its point of departure —an attack on unnatural "authors," authors in the Classical tradition, full of artifice ("goût artificiel" [*J.,* 114]),

[90] *Oeuvres de jeunesse,* ed. F. Deloffre (Paris: Gallimard, 1972), p. 692; hereafter referred to as "*O.j.*"

[91] *Journaux et oeuvres diverses,* eds. F. Deloffre and M. Gilot (Paris: Garnier, 1969), p. 118; hereafter referred to as "*J.*"

[92] Marivaux escapes from the frame of an English precedent only to be hounded by it infratextually, subliminally. This is typical.

"attention," "travail" (p. 115), and of the psychic distance this implies. It becomes a matter, for our narrator, of smashing intertextual mirrors, of upsetting in this instance the formal constraints of the "portrait" and its art of semiological surfaces, of descending into insides, his own and his objects' "sentiments": "Je me reprocherais d'écarter la situation d'esprit où je me trouve; je me livre aux sentiments qu'elle me donne, qui me pénètrent, et dont je voudrais pouvoir pénétrer les autres" (p. 127). His ideal is an abnegation of linguistic and ideological control or influence, a passive automatism that registers feeling and thought as they "surprise" him, without predetermined literary form: "je ne sais point créer, je sais seulement surprendre en moi les pensées que le hasard me fait, et je serais fâché d'y mettre rien du mien" (p. 114). He wavers, however, between "sentiments d'humanité" and "misanthropie" (pp. 117–18), occasions for sympathy and those that give the world and himself a comedic "caractère générique" (p. 132), the tension recurring throughout the *Journaux* in the frames (often frames within frames) that variously distance him from himself, his objects, and from other texts. Whichever distance he chooses, the eccentricity of his style cannot conceal flowers plucked from other gardens. To shake loose from the derivative, he imagines, out loud, a "libertinage d'idées" (p. 132), a now famous aesthetic disorder that violates classical progression and unity of tone or genre, an escape from shaping consciousness and repetitions such as one finds in the "Jardin du je ne sais quoi" (p. 348), Classicism's own more intimate or exotic shrubbery. It is, in his mind, the writing rather than the written, the mood of the pen scratching a continuously renewed present on the page, that offers the illusion of breaking the mirror, the "ceremonies" of past fiction and of what he himself has just written: "Pour moi, je ne sais pas comment j'écrirai: ce qui me viendra, nous l'aurons sans autre cérémonie; car je n'en sais pas d'autre que d'écrire tout couramment mes pensées" (p. 276). The sensuous wisdom or "volupté" of the narrator's *rapprochements* and of his *sensibilité* is here transferred to the Epicurean pleasure of attentive inattention, a studious closing in upon himself, "un plaisir d'écrire" (p. 276), in which the sins of outer-directed consciousness, vanity, wealth, and power are kept at bay—or so he hopes.

The "indigent philosophe," traveling (writing), like the narrator of *Pharsamon*, for "le plaisir du voyage" (*O.j.*, 457), leaves in his wake a pastiche of picaresque fiction, with intermittent bits of La Fontaine, Rabelais, La Rochefoucauld, and others. The naive and "natural" excursion of thought turns out to be, at least in part, a journey on the frontier of memory, and closeness to the self a closeness to an acculturated language that doesn't let off setting the narrator into frames of its (his) own making. The *philosophe* drinks, with reason, and his drinking invites a brilliant story of a drinking "camarade," the *philosophe*'s unnamed and unnameable double, who even more desperately tries to live in the unforeseeable, hating repetitions and commitments of all kinds. Every appearance or thing that *shows*, his face, his body, his picaresque narrative itself, distances him from being and makes of him a signifying and therefore vulnerable object for social intelligence, so that drinking (without which he cannot speak) becomes synonymous with the suspension of literary time, an authentic present in which the silent self, neither thinking nor doing, is unclassifiable: "les fous réfléchissent, et les sages font; et moi je bois: dans quelle classe suis-je? le proverbe n'en dit mot" (*J*, 294). It is the moment that precedes or interrupts but also inspires the inevitable frame of discourse, mask, and distance, a "riche parenthèse" (p. 292). Speaking, however, never stops; consciousness *appears* with it in the social "faces" of rhetoric, "noble" or "base," as Hegel would say, serving or reacting to "wealth and state power" and to its own exposure. Alcohol performs for these narrators, in respect to themselves, what "sentiment" does for them, in respect to others: it automatizes and integrates acts of consciousness—or pretends to. Yet these *rapprochements* force consciousness out of its shell and create in Marivaux's frames an even higher level of awareness that predicts Diderot's.

Imitative psychology, theories of "sentiment" and sympathetic imagination—long in practice before they appear in theory, culminating in Adam Smith and the Scottish philosophers[93]—hold forth the promise of an end to narrative frames, of a literature that one might describe as implosive, its persuasive power immanent, its language without surface and therefore irresistibly referential. They

[93] For theories of sympathetic imagination in England and Scotland, consult Walter Jackson Bate, *From Classic to Romantic* (Cambridge: Harvard University Press, 1949), Ch. 5. Nothing comparable exists for France.

look forward to the disappearance of authorial consciousness and the memory of texts past and so to the destruction
of what Rousseau will call "les maximes des grandes
sociétés."[94] The Classical art of distance had been an art of
conspiracy and condescension, "l'art de faire sa cour au
plus fort" (I, 24), the strongest prevailing ideology, aesthetic,
and social system; the author's rhetorical stance a pass-
port to "la bonne compagnie"; his particular brand of
"reason" self-serving and exclusionary. Vauvenargues,
before mid-century, spent his short literary life trying to
bend Classical forms to accommodate disenfranchised
emotions and a new "sympathetic" social vision: his
"maximes" are languorous and almost without wit: his
"caractères," detailed, ungeneralized descriptions of particular men in their unnoticed suffering, samples of the new
"realism," portraits of the unconventional and irreducible,
who cannot be put in their place, tagged by the usual social
labels.[95] But if the stabilized consciousness of Classicism
struggles to fuse with its object in acts of sympathetic
imagination, it discovers, as Protos confided to Lafcadio,
that one cannot leave one society "sans tomber du même
coup dans une autre." Ever sensitive to power relationships, Marivaux (especially in *Marianne*) and then Diderot,
and to a certain extent Voltaire, explore the new consciousness and notice that it too is a strategy—the politics of

[94]"Seconde Préface" to *La Nouvelle Héloïse*, in *Oeuvres complètes*, eds.
B. Gagnebin and M. Raymond (Paris: Gallimard, 1959–), I, 22.
[95]See my article, "Vauvenargues and the Whole Truth," *PMLA*, 85
(October 1970), 1106–15.

transcendence exchanged for the arguably more manipu-lative, personal, and idiosyncratic politics of immanence. In Diderot, who arrives somewhat later on the scene and who, by virtue of background and temperament, is far less wary than the others, the new consciousness operates from the start. He grows aware of the exercise of power, its shameful possibilities as well as its impossibilities, only after he has exuberantly exploited it. In the *Salon* of 1767—to offer only that example because it is most explicit and occurs in a contextual power play that blankets it—Diderot can cynically write: "on a mis en jeu notre sensibilité; nous montrons cette sensibilité; c'est une si belle qualité!" (A-T, X, 25).

Diderot's narratives of the 60's and 70's *test* the pleasures and vulnerabilities, the moral point and moral failings of this consciousness, with the frames I've already described, frames that recast mimetic propositions into ironic ones by creating a bewildering authorial suspensiveness, a benumbed perception of the world's and the mind's own disjunctions, a metaphysics of irony.[96] I want here, before passing on to

---

[96]See Sharon L. Kabelac, "Irony as Metaphysics in *Le Neveu de Rameau*," *Diderot Studies*, 14 (1971), 97–112. For a theoretical elucida-tion of the entire question of irony as vision rather than technique and for the term "suspensive irony," consult Alan Wilde, "Modernism" (cited in note 73, above) and "Barthelme Unfair to Kierkegaard: Some Thoughts on Modern and Postmodern Irony," *boundary 2*, 5 (Fall 1976), 45–70. See also D. C. Muecke's *The Compass of Irony* (London: Methuen & Co., 1969), Ch. VI.

Julia Kristeva, in "La Musique parlée ou remarques sur la subjectivité dans la fiction, à propos du 'Neveu de Rameau,'" published in *Langue et*

Rousseau, only to dare correct Hegel, who offers us Rameau as the herald of brighter days, a new, "self-estranged" consciousness, alienated from himself and society. Hegel admires Rameau both for his self-consciousness, "this self that is turned into a thing," and its dialectical extension, "self-lessness."[97] And when he cites his two examples from the *Neveu* of the "style of speech" of these consciousnesses, he uses episodes of Rameau's mimicry: "this style of speech is the madness of the musician" (p. 543). It is hard to imagine how this "style" can deliver the "universal talk and depreciatory judgment" of "spirit truly

---

langages de Leibniz à l'Encyclopédie, eds. Michèle Duchet and Michèle Jalley (Paris: Union Générale d'Editions, 1977), pp. 153–206, comes closest to describing the multivalent poise of Diderot's authorial (un)consciousness, a (non-)subjectivity, a "sujet pluralisé" (p. 166) that is "le procès sémiotique de lui-même" (p. 164). Her breathtaking structuralist and Freudian analysis stresses beginnings, the "mise en procès" (p. 165) of this consciousness and therefore the "pulsions" that inhabit it. The etiology of authorial consciousness is not the whole of it, and the automatisms of "production" do not perhaps offer the best models for an operation that corrects and revises itself reactively and in process or years later—which is why neither "consciousness" nor "unconsciousness," "subjectivity" nor "non-subjectivity" is totally adequate to describe an authorial presence or vision that we can only construct (interpret) from the sum of all its semiotic parts and not simply from those that propose an ideological subversion. For this reason, the Hegelian notion of irony as negativity (negation of the self, of the natural and political order) presides over Kristeva's text (p. 154) and leaves no room for the suspensive irony produced by the joint force and full result of all the text's voices.

[97] *The Phenomenology of Mind,* tr. J. B. Baillie (London: George Allen & Unwin, 1961), p. 542.

objective," since Rameau's frenzy is a superb example of imitative sympathy, light miles away from the "scornful laughter" (p. 546) he (or Hegel's "Spirit") elsewhere pours on existence and on him- or itself.[98] If my perspective serves, the mocking and self-mocking Rameau has his source not in a new consciousness, which does indeed thrive on "self-lessness," but in the "universal talk and depreciatory judgment" of the older, rebellious conscious-ness and self-consciousness we find in Marivaux's drunkard, who is socialized but alienated from his socialization. The madness of Rameau's style, by which Hegel means its mixture of high and low, parodies of the grotesque and the exalted, can also be found in this drunkard, whose "self-lessness," we recall, is locked in his bottle. To be, then, more historical about what is or isn't a new consciousness, one would have to say that MOI, the "moral sense" philoso-pher, and the narrative voice, for all the vagaries of their distance, and Diderot's own later strictures on Hutcheson for not being "experimental" enough, come closer than Rameau to the new.[99] By this time, the new is actually

[98]See Lionel Trilling's strictures on Hegel's reading of Rameau in *Sincerity and Authenticity* (Cambridge: Harvard University Press, 1972). Trilling helps my argument by noticing that Rameau's performance "is not scornful, but, rather, charged with admiration and love of the human and natural phenomena it represents" (p. 46).

[99]Just how old or prevalent Rameau's insolence, deprecation, and protective self-consciousness were can be inferred, in part, from a passage in Duclos' *Considérations sur les moeurs de ce siècle* (1750), a summation of contemporary manners written at least ten years before the *Neveu* and intended to capture the spirit of the entire century at

several decades old and has all the marks of social acceptance. For which it too is on trial, its self-lessness modulating into self-consciousness.

The most desperate movement of consciousness and therefore, in this schematic tableau, the last, does not belong to Diderot, but to Rousseau, whose tormented frames magnify every authorial anxiety I've touched upon—anxieties of power, language, repetition, and distance. Rousseau's frames may seem at first difficult to locate, except of course for those his prefaces and footnotes supply. This is because the narrative voice, insisting on its temporal dimension (the present), creates a frame around the (its) past. The frame acts as a metaphor of distance, and though we are used to this narrative device

---

midpoint. The passage is never mentioned and is yet so strikingly apposite—even in its evocation of the analogy of a chess match—that it deserves to be read at length: "On se cachoit autrefois de certains procédés, et l'on rougissoit s'ils venoient à se découvrir. Il me semble qu'on les a aujourd'hui trop ouvertement, et dès-là il doit s'en trouver davantage, parce que la contrainte et la honte retenoient bien des hommes . . . Un homme d'un caractère leste trouve encore alors le secret de n'être pas déshonoré [d'une action blâmable], s'il a le courage d'être le premier à le publier, et de plaisanter ceux qui seroient tentés de le blâmer. On n'ose plus la lui reprocher, quand on le voit en faire gloire. L'audace fait sa justification, et le reproche qu'on lui feroit seroit un ridicule auquel on n'ose s'exposer . . . dans les moeurs, prévenir un reproche, c'est le détruire . . . Un homme qui en a trompé un autre . . . loin d'en avoir des remords ou de la honte, se félicite sur son habilité . . . il s'imagine simplement avoir gagné une belle partie d'échecs" (ed. F. C. Green [Cambridge: Cambridge University Press, 1946], pp. 58–60.

in Crébillon, Marivaux, and others, the estrangement from the past has in Rousseau a vast, slowly measured, and calamitous diachrony that imitates not simply the socialization of consciousness but the bitter progress of history. In works from the two *Discours*, the *Nouvelle Héloïse*, and *Emile*, to the *Rêveries*, narrators and writing itself contend with the *mistake* that gave rise to their necessity, a mistake that is even at the moment of narration being repeated. The narrator's first "I" closes a circle of imploded "I's," which flow outward, from past to present, like the fitful but unconscious transition from sleep to wakefulness.[100] From the hypothesized and distanced center to the circumference of narrative, there is—we're told, or it is implied—a depletion of energy and value that results in this final social exposure. Consciousness bites its tail and hopes not to be trampled; it hopes in fact to disappear, or to feign death.[101]

[100] I borrow this image from *Emile,* in which Rousseau speaks of "la continuité d'un paisible sommeil" (IV, 376) that has to be interrupted for the Stoic training of the child, just as every "plénitude de vie" (p. 419), every unconscious or imaginary arrest in time must break into the lumpy aridity of disenchantment or wakefulness.

[101] I am avoiding the term "transparency" here and in my subsequent discussion. Jean Starobinski is so convincing in his *Jean-Jacques Rousseau. La Transparence et l'obstacle* (Paris: Plon, 1958) that he is likely to shunt all thought away from the issue. Though I come at the same phenomenon from a more structural and aesthetic point of view, I happily acknowledge my debt to this most provocative of living critics and to others who sponsor the notion of an "unmediated presence" in Rousseau. The entire question of a rhetoric of invisibility deserves further study and must, I think, be set in the historical perspective of an Augustinian tradition of "eloquence," as described by Joseph A. Mazzeo

Rousseau contrives secret, impregnable spaces for its display, beginning with the first and second *Discours,* using in both, as the canon Gautier, his contemporary, noticed in the first, a "pompe oratoire,"[102] an archaic and academic *oral* rhetoric, alternately officious and pedantic, situating the narrative voice in what is assumed to be an unbroken tradition now worn thin. It is intended, in every way, to be a voice from the ancient past that will survive "au-delà de son

---

in a chapter of his book, *Renaissance and Seventeenth-Century Studies* (New York: Columbia University Press, 1964), called "St. Augustine's Rhetoric of Silence: Truth vs. Eloquence and Things vs. Signs," an eloquence perpetuated in France not only by Port-Royal and its literary wing (see Jean Lafond's recent, magisterial study, *La Rochefoucauld: Augustinisme et Littérature* (Paris: Klincksieck, 1977), but particularly by Fénelon, in his *Dialogues sur l'éloquence en général et sur celle de la chaire en particulier* and the better known *Lettre à l'Académie.* Augustinian "silence" expresses the desire to circumvent all sensuous mediation, linguistic and personal. Rousseau was most susceptible to this tradition and used it for his own ends, but it is a mistake to believe, as some do, that he invented it, just as it is equally wrong to think that Rousseau was alone in espousing its ideal. In people like Condillac and Diderot the tradition is far more covert, but one can even discover it in Voltaire (about whom, see the searching article by Julia L. Epstein, "Voltaire's Ventriloquism: Voices in the First *Lettre philosophique,*" soon to appear in *Studies on Voltaire and the Eighteenth Century*). The perpetual renewal of Augustinian rhetoric as it manifests itself in this new eighteenth-century wave has to do, I believe, with the slow but steady swell of imitative sympathy and sentimentality—the desire for a new cohesiveness and referential immediacy —not only in fiction, but in the sciences, philosophy, and theology, to the extent that these can be separated.

[102] In his letter to Grimm, "sur la réfutation de son Discours," Rousseau accuses Gautier of the same "pompe oratoire" (III, 65).

siècle" (III, 3), impersonal in its imitated *humanitas*. Fabricius's famous harangue is only an intensification of this voice, lustier and more extravagantly rhetorical as it touches home ground, its own past. But Fabricius, as Robert Ellrich pointed out, returns after his own death to an Imperial Rome, to people "now strangers to him,"[103] and so he too, like the narrator-"citoyen de Genève," is a "virtuous outsider"—a stern, yet spectral voice from a better past, a specifically oral survivor, beyond physical reach. Here, as in the second *Discours,* which is delivered within the fictional enclosure of the "lycée d'Athènes," the narrative frame creates a series of temporal Chinese boxes or sound systems that make the same noise, the one most deeply enclosed setting the pitch for the others. The narrator's language certifies its own inevitability, a lonely and self-conscious remainder of what has always been immanent, though dead to most, a language which, however academic it may have appeared and still appears to Rousseau's readers, is meant to suggest not the dust or deception but the living fire of illusion, bookish illusion from ancient historians to Classical and contemporary "dialogues of the dead." He sets himself beneath their shield and their other-worldly "truth." It is worth noting, since I'm here touching on Rousseau's use of a literary canon, the remarkable inversion—one of a series of inversions—that his narrators effectuate from the start,

[103]*Rousseau and his Reader: the Rhetorical Situation of the Major Works,* University of North Carolina Studies in the Romance Languages and Literatures, 8 (Chapel Hill: University of North Carolina Press, 1969), 28.

but with increasing intransigence as they progress: the ideal forms of these fictions, heretofore a trap for the unwary imitator, become the signs of an incipient and lurking truth; and the shrouded and so protected quality of fiction itself suggests the defensive form or level of consciousness for any present or future discourse. In this inversion, the narrative frame, which used to rope us off from a "fictitious" life, crowding us into an elevated space of suspicion, tries instead to imply that it is our outer space that is illusory.

The "phraseological" frame (Uspensky's term) of the second *Discours*, the present use of the supposed language of the Ancients, indicates how internalized their imaginary truth has become. And just as history in the second *Discours* loses all transcendent direction and becomes a story whose plot is always immanent and accidental, the mysteriously disturbed growth and unfolding of an embryonic unit, disastrously reaching out for "suppléments"[104] and visibility ("moral" sight and being seen), so the narrator, who claims to have found truth not in books ("non dans les livres") but in himself, cannot locate the outside disturbance of literature and insists rather on the immanence of his expressivity, its continuity with the past, and, finally, its regrettable visibility. Already in the preamble to the *Discours*, the narrator wants to "appear" as an invisible mediator of an internal speech, a cyclist who doesn't use his hands: "il n'y aura de faux que ce que j'y aurai mêlé du

---

[104]See Jacques Derrida, *De la grammatologie* (Paris: Les Editions de Minuit, 1967), *passim*.

mien sans le vouloir" (p. 70)—which of course reminds us of Marivaux's: "je serais fâché d'y mettre rien du mien." In both cases, we are on the brink of a new aesthetic and a new use of frames—their impossible object, to remove any distance between consciousness, socially, which is to say, linguistically, aware, and the innate energies of the story it has to tell.

Rousseau's narrators are thereafter to proclaim themselves the survivors of a consciousness effaced in its seamless dream—the solipsistic dream of Emile's early life, reproduced in the "dream" of *Emile*,[105] or of Julie and Saint-Preux's dream of love, sublimated and obscured in their watchful life at Clarens, and of Jean-Jacques's own tranquil ecstasies in the *Rêveries*. All dreams of the cooperation of consciousness and its object, Rousseau's powerful version of imitative sympathy—an "identification" with sensations, natural elements and scenes, "le matérialisme du sage"; or with romance, epic and love poetry, the materialism of the reader; or with other personalities, the materialism of "charme," elective affinities. Whether or not these sympathies can be said to be wholly subjective or phenomenological,[106] they discharge inner or outer

[105] In a footnote, Rousseau, attacking all science as a dream, comments: "on me dira que je rêve aussi; j'en conviens . . . je donne mes rêves pour des rêves" (IV, 351).

[106] Since Rousseau insists on the cooperation of insides and outsides, often on the fact that nature and our natures, like history, are "novels" through which we live, the dreamer dreamed, our version of life in or out of tune with a silent but overpowering melody, his work inscribed within the sound, I see no point in denying him contact with the

vibrations, "felt in the blood and felt along the heart," or projected into instinctive imitations, symbolically reproduced in our behavior or in figures of sound, gesture, and language—the last, Rousseau warns in the *Essai sur l'origine des langues,* "less happily"[107] because less expressive, more conventionally mediated and consciously externalized. The seams that grieve his narrators most are seams of time, the fissure of consciousness awaking to "cette force intelligente qui *superpose* et puis qui prononce" (*Emile,* IV, 571; my italics) and therefore seams of language, its signifiers arising belatedly to float in "formes déterminées" (*Emile,* IV, 686) above a lost sensation, feeling, or image. For God, for Rousseau during his reveries, and in that palimpsest emblem of perfect confinement and framing, Julie's Elysian garden, whose boundaries are invisible, "les temps n'ont point de succession" (II, 673)—a temporal seamlessness to inhabit a spatial one. Those who enter these narcotic realms of consciousness or art do so in the manner of the Englishman Robert Harbison describes, stumbling over a ha-ha, the sunken fence dividing his English garden from the rest of his grounds, "without realizing he is in a garden at all, like someone who misses an irony."[108] In

---

horizons of empirical reality *as he sees it,* however internalized and imaginary. If the imaginary is real for Rousseau, as Marc Eigeldinger claims, who can furnish proof that Rousseau is wrong? And what ought to interest us is not this shell of illusion, which can only lead to the Nietzschean impasse explored by Paul de Man, but the cooperative processes of subject and object within it.

[107](Paris: Bibliothèque du Graphe, n.d.), p. 501.

[108]*Eccentric Spaces* (New York: Alfred A. Knopf, 1977), p. 5.

Rousseau's Utopian and anironic city, time moves without jolts, "ni secousses ni intervalles" (*Rêveries,* I, 1047), the invisible spirit of things imprisons us in "le beau roman . . . de la nature humaine" (*Emile,* IV, 777), engrossing us in its "fiction" (truth), read in our senses or imagination. Like Julie's birds, beguiled by an illusion of freedom, or Julie herself, or Emile, we are caged in the degradation of time (death) and history, repeating[109] what was foretold, the fiction of truth or the truth of fiction, Abelard and Eloise, *Robinson Crusoe,* Petrarch, or *Télémaque,* beneath the eye of some non-human or invisible conscience—not our own.

"L'heure sonne, quel changement! A l'instant son oeil se ternit, sa gaieté s'efface" (IV, 419)—so the narrator of *Emile,* the celebrated invisible hand and eye, manipulating and watching that "insect in the center of its web" (p. 305), his pupil, the narrator such as he was. As children smash the injured toys they love, Rousseau's narrators punish their subjects (themselves) for their expansion into consciousness and make necessity a crime, the crime of a seamed or framed narration as well as the crime of leaving the "springtime" of life. If there certainly is, as Derrida says, a guilty onanism in the act of writing (p. 235), and imagination has "le pouvoir . . . de s'affecter elle-même de sa propre re-présentation" (p. 261), this publishable onanism

---

[109]For repetitions as a structural principle in *La Nouvelle Héloïse,* though not principally imitative ones, see Godelieve Mercken-Spaas, "La Répétition à la deuxième puissance," *Studies in Eighteenth-Century Culture,* 5 (Madison: University of Wisconsin Press, 1976); for repetitions, these more imitative, see David L. Anderson, "Aspects of Motif in *La Nouvelle Héloïse,*" *Studies on Voltaire and the Eighteenth Century,* 44 (1972).

and imagination are unnaturally conscious, and conscious too of the uselessness of their gestures, which are gestures *about* an image of onanism and so filled with the mortal sadness that, for Rousseau, kills sexuality. There seems little doubt, in any case, that the far greater felony and embarrassment is coitus, the introduction of a visible discourse into the social world, proving, in the end, that those rhythms are best that resemble the bare, regular, and inaudible sounds of a heartbeat—Paul de Man's "successive repetition," "a movement that is bound to remain endless,"[110] more akin to post-coital disengagement; its objective correlative, the lapping waves of the lac de Bienne. A chronological reading of Rousseau, who is constantly reframing his preceding works as irremediable encounters with society and so reliving through their exposure the stages of awareness that characterize human evolution, makes it appear that the original sin, Rousseau's

[110]*Blindness and Insight* (New York: Oxford University Press, 1971), p. 129. Paul de Man transforms every quest in Rousseau into a quest for pure successivity, the "successive projection of a single moment of radical contradiction—the present" (p. 132). Narrative chronology becomes the "structural correlative of the necessarily figural nature of language" (p. 133), and its content is, strictly speaking, meaning-less. I do not know whether this cool interpretation is less "accompanied by an overtone of intellectual or moral superiority" (p. 112) de Man detects in all other critics, who, he claims, haven't been reading Rousseau's own statements attentively enough. But his complex, tightly-argued nihilism and reflexive referentiality deprives Rousseau of all power to "represent," to speak meaningfully *about* empirical reality and, incidentally, about himself, his own empirical past, in the *Confessions,* for example, or the *Rêveries*. It will surprise nobody nowadays that all writing and all history

kiss in the garden, was the first and second *Discours*—after which, the rest was *forcé*, a repetition without ecstasy: "Je n'eus qu'un moment," he writes in the *Préface* to the *Lettre à d'Alembert sur les spectacles*, "il est passé; j'ai la honte de me survivre."[111] If he is henceforth to have a purpose and a "point," he must seem utterly passive, all "passions éteintes" (first version, p. 190), a man dying or, like Fabricius, dead: "car pour moi, je ne suis plus" (p. 10), his pen dipped in disappearing ink, driven by a careless and digressive mind, obeying its own rhythms. All of Rousseau's prefaces and frames will now suggest the same: a "persuasion intérieure" instead of a "tour persuasif" (second Preface, *Nouvelle Héloïse*, II, 14), the work of "un homme qui n'est plus," (*Ebauches des Confessions*, I, 1159) "sans ordre et presque sans suite," (Preface, *Emile*, IV, 241) a

---

is fiction of a kind, and Rousseau helped lay, we might say, the foundation of this belief, but what will de Man do with Rousseau's claim to "truth," a prospective, intersubjective, and, as Starobinski explains, a generalized truth, the truth of fiction or the truth of his experience? The "elegiac tone" (p. 133) of so many of Rousseau's narrative frames does in fact both "express a nostalgia for an original presence" *and* serves as a "purely dramatic device." The example de Man offers, from the second *Discours*, of Rousseau's confession within the text, if not of a "deluded primitivism" (p. 133, n. 41) then of an imagined one, has to be offset by other examples from the *Lettre à d'Alembert*, the *Confessions*, and the *Rêveries*—texts slighted by de Man—in which the past is palpable enough, regretted, and "represented." Nostalgia is not always, in Rousseau, deprived "of all foundation," unless one picks and chooses among his theories and fictions and then mercilessly spreads the densely coordinated yield over all of Rousseau's narratives.

[111]Ed. M. Fuchs (Geneva: Droz, 1948), p. 10.

rhetoric in which there is "rien de saillant" (second Preface, *Nouvelle Heloïse*, II, 15). Nothing, in short, that threatens or asserts itself (*dejectum membrum*)—at least in these conscious credos, which affirm their *frontlessness*, an inverted form of the backlessness of earlier narrative strategies, however similar their aesthetic of disorder. In Rousseau's prefaces and in his later fiction, we see backs bent over their work, backs so absorbed and vulnerable that we dare not strike. Our attention is transferred, it is hoped, to what they are saying and imitating.

Though Marivaux and Diderot also request this generosity, in Rousseau the doctrine of sympathetic imitation, its power to implode consciousness, to cancel transcendence (distance), to establish a symbiotic complicity with a surrounding linguistic, plastic, or moral space, reveals itself most fully and consistently as a self-protective tactic. He pushes to its furthest limit what is perhaps inevitable in certain doctrines of immanence: by taking its object out of the sky and then, further, out of the world, and by placing it in the reflexivity of the self, it imposes on consciousness the task of a private speech that is also pregnant with universality. (As a solution to Classical and post-Classical egocentric divisiveness, which hangs in the iron grip of a regulated, universal discourse, the ideology of immanence, battling for a new, more cohesive society, inverts the terms of the old arrangement and paradoxically, though deliberately, produces an individualistic discourse.) And what was once a distance from the object outside reappears as the distance of consciousness from its interiorized treasure. How to protect this treasure without protecting its container—the metonymy of the speaker? In Rousseau, who senses this necessity most because he most internalizes the problem, both the despair of external attack and the anguish of separation from his internal object become a lifetime's haunting. The assumption of a rational and linguistic perspective involves not only the embarrassment of exposure, but a horrible deprivation, the loss of moral, organic immediacy and an impotent longing, mixed with guilt, anger, or envy, for the snug coextension of consciousness and its remembered pleasure or truth. The more Rousseau advances backward toward these, the further they seem to recede, reversing the human dash through history, in which the more we run, the more we are pursued.

The specificity of consciousness in Rousseau's frames can only be measured by their mournful distance from what they bracket—a distance constantly renewed by the intensity of their desire to disappear, to identify unutterably with their object. (The Romantics will of course rediscover that separations of subject and object grow worse by virtue of the fury with which one tries to overcome them.) The new imitative consciousness gives birth to this exacerbated consciousness of distance from itself, from language, and from the world and so also to an irony of reflexiveness, which surveys the disjunctive landscape of the self and its instruments, an irony without windows or sunshine, but one that has maintained a remarkably enduring novelty to this day. Diderot will never dwell here for long or consent to remain stuck at this level, though he can understand and portray it. If the new consciousness results in the new metonymic importance of the author, as I've suggested, and selling one's product, one's vulgarization, translation, or imitation invariably becomes the merchandizing of its sympathetic creator, packaged into it, Diderot, who grows weary or frightened of confinement, as Rousseau does not, will forever leap from his box. Consciousness in Diderot is everywhere at a crossroad: no path is untried. But he is too mercurial and self-critical, too attuned to the old sense of ridicule and irony, too sociable, jocular, and demystifying not to enjoy as well as bemoan the aftermath of sympathy, the "délassement" of overarching himself and others. If consciousness rises in mid-century only after it has invested itself, it seeks always some social and personal profit from its investment, but only in Rousseau does it long permanently to drown.

Appendix of Translations

18 —Please note that the issue is religion in general

20 —to communicate to others the pleasure one feels

21 —echo through the centuries
    —beneath the eyes of the divinity
    —this contemplation which annihilates him

22 —possible beings, consisting of body and spirit like ourselves

23 —the real and true scene
    —it is only, so to speak, the translation of it
    —I would like painters, poets, to instruct, inspire, and excite one
    another; and this borrowing of light and inspiration is not
    plagiarism.

24 —the spirit of the thing

25 —It all comes down to shuttling from the senses to reflection and
    from reflection to he senses: alternately and repeatedly
    returning home to oneself and going out the door. It is bee's
    work . . . One makes lots of piles of wax if one isn't able to
    generate rays of light in the process.
    —The inspired person is himself uncertain whether what he
    asserts is real or chimerical, whether it ever existed outside of
    himself. At this point, he is at the outer limit of nature and man,
    and at the furthest reaches of the resources of art.

26 —the same impression in the soul of the reader
    —you, who are the final object, the end of all writing

27 —he perorates, they listen, hanging from his lips. He is a somebody.

28 —Let every public man avoid that discretion which is so opposed
    to the progress of knowledge! One must reveal both the thing
    and the manner of doing it.

29 —It struck me that one would have to be simultaneously inside
    and outside oneself, be both observer and the mechanism
    observed. But the mind is like the eye: it cannot watch itself
    watching.

31 —here, exposing to the censor the philosopher behind whom I
    keep myself concealed; there, assuming the opposite position

and exposing myself to arrows that will only wound Seneca, concealed behind me.

32   —[the] "ivy" [to Batteux's] "oak"
—If my ideas happened to be close to yours, they are like the ivy that occasionally mixes its foliage with the leaves of the oak it entwines.

33   —sensitive to every charm . . . capable of an infinite number of different enthusiasms

34   —the more one details, the more the image one presents to others differs from the one on the canvas
—one takes a few steps up to this vase . . .
—Enter, and you will see on the right . . .
—How innocent she is!

34-35—She is beginning to think: her heart is starting to flutter, and it will soon pound.

35   —This child is weeping over something else, I tell you.
—Admiration embraces and hugs unthinkingly the thing it admires or the thing it beholds.
—[like sympathy] which presses and fastens two beings together
—And how that sweet softness takes hold of you and slides along the veins of the viewer as he watches it undulate in the contours of her body

36   —and the curve of those hips! those buttocks! and those thighs! those knees! those legs

36-37—the soul of a large mannequin, which envelops it

37   —Aren't you tired of wandering around this huge salon?
—it is you who made me walk here, you're the one who led me about

38   —from one language to another the spots one understands best
—the pleasure of being my own master, the pleasure of recognizing my own goodness, the pleasure of seeing myself and taking delight in it, the even sweeter pleasure of forgetting myself
—as from some fertile ground

39 —farewell my divine existence . . . Would that she were here now . . .
    —Why am I alone here? Why isn't there anyone to share with me the charm, the loveliness of this site? . . . A certain feeling is missing.

43 —I only listen for the pleasure of telling it to someone else
    —without witness and without result

44 —to make himself understandable to me, Cléobule had used terms and comparisons from my art
    —According to the key, it is Ariste; according to the sense, it would probably be Cléobule.
    —a bit in the European manner

45 —I would really like to know what you think of these people.

45-46—There is therefore a contradiction in the texture of the narration itself, between a tendency to yield to what I would call the *tyranny of the subject* and the opposite tendency to objectify the narrative material.

47 —starting with facts, they ended with reflections

48 —made me write a piece
    —a thing's return in the direction from which it came

48-49—all kinds of reverberations and spurtings

49 —supplement refers to the addition one makes to something to supply what is lacking in it
    —to put one thing in place of another that is missing

50 —A. Do you really believe in this fable about Tahiti? / B. It isn't a fable; and you wouldn't doubt the sincerity of Bougainville if you were familiar with the supplement to his voyage.
    —It is an old man who speaks
    —When Bougainville's boat approached Tahiti
    —They threw him provisions . . . they grabbed the men . . . they stretched forth their arms; they caught hold of ropes; they climbed planks
    —less than he might

52 —Skip this preamble, which means nothing, and go straight on to the farewell address one of the chiefs of the island delivered to our travelers

54 —The act of generalizing tends to strip concepts of their palpable content. As this act progresses, all corporeal residues disappear; notions withdraw slowly from the imagination as they move toward understanding; and ideas become purely intellectual. Then the speculative philosopher resembles the man who looks down from one of those mountain tops that are lost in the clouds: the objects on the plain below have disappeared; he is now left with only the spectacle of his own thoughts and the consciousness of the height to which he has ascended and where not everyone can follow or breathe.

56 —You see that the nature of tropes or figures is to make images by giving body and movement to all our ideas.

57 —that kind of metaphor which, in order to supply thought with color and make an object palpable, if it is not sufficiently so, paints a picture of it using characteristics that are not its own but belong to an analogous object
—the faculty of attaching a body to an abstract word [. . .] the faculty of borrowing from sensuous objects images that serve for comparison

65 —it shows none

66 —a pact whose mystery must be revealed; and it can never be revealed completely, because there are, in language, delicate nuances which remain necessarily indeterminate
—more attentive and penetrating *glances*

67 —what was once new . . . the direct observation of the external world

68 —They have so often and so closely viewed nature in its operations
—the dreams of a sick person
—it is such a precarious unity

69 —the observations or experiments that stemmed from it
—abstract and general sounds

69   —knowledge advancing from its soul toward objects by the very path it used in first observing these objects

70   —Retraces the past, anticipates the future,/ Remakes all that was, makes all that must be,/ Beckons the latter to exist, the former to be reborn.

71   —a violent movement of the soul by which we are transported into the midst of objects that we are to represent; then we see scenes taking place in our imagination as if they were outside us: they are there in fact, for as long as this illusion lasts, all existing things are eradicated, and our ideas spring up to replace them: all we perceive are our ideas . . . If this state isn't madness, it is very close to it. That is why one needs a good deal of sense to counterbalance enthusiasm.

72   —The imaginative man strolls about in his head like someone snooping about in a palace . . . he goes hither and yon, he never leaves.
  —Imagination creates nothing, it imitates, it compares, combines, exaggerates, diminishes
  —The reign of images passes as the reign of things spreads its dominion

73   —the image of a nature separate from man but drawn to his measure and the measure of his reactions

75   —ordinarily see what is in front of their eyes and see only that
  —We use reasons

75-76—two good eyes are all one needs to proceed correctly

76   —her reasons better than she had first imagined

77   —some fixed point in space . . . from which one might declare the truth to *them*

78   —I am surer of my judgment than of my eyes.

79   —Blindness must, at first, have been used to describe only a loss of eyesight; but anyone who does not clearly see ideas and their relations, whose reason is disturbed or obscured, is he not a little like the *blind man* who does not see physical objects? The word *blindness* naturally came to mind to express this loss of mental sight as well.

160

81 —So much do our virtues depend on our manner of feeling and on the extent to which external things affect us!

83 —is always external to us, foreign, produced by an agent or by some cause which is not us
—any motive, be it external or internal, is independent of us

84 —unless he can forget and distract himself
—it is no longer the thinker who acts, it is the spirit of someone else that controls him

88 —Let us together fly to the confines of this universe, beyond the mere point to which I am confined.

89 —our imagination has less scruples than our eyes

90 —fine and subtle analogies, which summon objects together on a canvas and which bind them with secret, imperceptible threads

91 —all things are in a chain
—mountains whose summits are lost in the clouds
—the consciousness of the height he has reached

92 —how metaphoric is the language of gestures!
—which is what happens all the time in society
—a single perception of the soul
—impressions in their entirety and simultaneously
—are only signs of our ideas
—words are and can only be signs approximating thoughts, feelings, ideas

93 —at the moment understanding grasps them, the soul is stirred, imagination sees them, and our ears hear them

94 —a natural order of ideas that pre-exist in one's mind, quite the opposite of the order of expression

96 —here they softened an expression, there they palliated a feeling; elsewhere they led up to an incident

98 —That is neither verisimilar nor true.
—Beloved, who was then so dear to me
—we would be truly unfortunate if there were no woman in society who resembled her

100 —There are expressions, thoughts, that are less hers than yours.

102 —Dorval had attempted, without success, to bring an end to a dispute that had been dividing two families in the neighborhood.
—He was dejected over it, and I sensed that this unhappy frame of mind was going to cast a dark shadow over our discussion.

103 —we must be wholly focusing on the same thing
—he who acts and he who looks on are two different beings
—close to daily experience

104 —I stalked the emotions his face registered; and I began to share his ecstasy, when suddenly I cried out, almost in spite of myself: "He has fallen beneath the spell."

105 —It is true. Here is where one sees nature. Here is the sacred dwelling place of enthusiasm. If a man has genius, he leaves the city and its inhabitants
—pour forth a torrent of ideas that rush ahead, collide, and scatter
—A silence fell between us

106 —Who joins the sound of his voice to the sound of waters rushing down the mountainside?
—O Nature, all that is good is enclosed in your bosom. You are the fertile source of all truths.

110 —After tremendous effort, there is a kind of relaxation one finds irresistible and which you would be familiar with if the exercise of virtue had been painful to you. You never felt the need to breathe . . . I was enjoying my victory. I forced the worthiest feelings from my friend's heart; he became even worthier of what I had done for him. And this action doesn't seem natural to you!

112 —the number of different ways of viewing things is almost infinite, and nature itself is truly so

115 —Poet, are you sensitive and discerning? Pluck this string, and you will hear it resound or quiver in every soul.
—According to some modern speculators, everything in the arts ought to contrive to yield what they call an *effect,* that is, the greatest illusion and emotion.

119 —we joined her, our souls trembled, and we shared her rapture
—I interrupted her, or I spoke her words before she could, or we spoke together

119   —I was shut in my cell; silence was imposed on me; I was separated from everyone, left to myself

      —My friend, I'm tired of this awful place. Life evaporates here. Nothing gets done.

120   —those enormous balloons that float or remain suspended in the atmosphere [and which] remain there like lumps of sugar at the bottom of a cup of coffee, which can't absorb any more of it.

121   —decency unites their opinions, fuses them, makes them one

      —this happiness that assimilated us

122   —it emanates from a soft, insensate, inert substance which serves as its pillow

124   —No more, no more confidence in a man who can feign so truthfully

      —I can't get over so long a resentment, a pack of tricks and lies that lasts for almost a year.

      —Nor I, nor Jacques, nor his master, nor the hostess.

      —*written* on high

129   —the shape of our novel

131   —They do not try to adapt their language to the world, but to subjugate the world to their mental system.

133   —beautiful without knowing it

134   —I would reproach myself for overlooking my present state of mind; I want to give myself up to the feelings it bestows, feelings that move me and by which I would like others to be moved.

      —I am not able to create, I only know how to catch random thoughts as if by surprise, and I would be sorry to add anything of my own.

135   —As for me, I'm not sure how I will write: we will have what occurs to me without further ado or ceremony; for I know no other way of writing than to transcribe my thoughts as they come to me.

136   —fools reflect, and wise men do; and me, I drink. To which class do I belong? the proverb is silent on this score.

137   —the art of courting the strongest

Translation of Notes

3 —Translation was never more than an early phase for the future philosopher and Encyclopedist. His true vocation is that of the vulgarizer, in the best sense of the word. Nothing illustrates this vocation better than his reaction to the translation of Shaftesbury.

7 —He marries himself to his subjects. He enters and inseminates them.

8 —no one has ever used anybody else's property with so much license

10 —suspended above all human considerations, and hovering above the atmosphere . . . It is from this position that I have really been able to shout, "I am free," and to feel equal to [at the level of] my subject matter.
   —Fragment by fragment, Diderot was able to fashion this discourse *about* history, a discourse which finds its unity in the very discourse in which it lodges.

11 —One has to settle for watching the author . . . address now the sovereign powers of the world, now the mongrels of literature and, in his dramatic enthusiasm . . . apostrophize himself, apostrophize his readers and indeed leave them the impossible task of discovering which character is speaking and which he is addressing.
   —the language of others
   —a willed self-alienation

14 —There is, then, only one way of faithfully translating a foreign author into our language: it is to have one's soul filled with impressions we have received from him and only to be satisfied with one's translation when it arouses the same impressions in the reader's soul.

17 —I confess that it is useless for me to wonder, since both reason and experience have made it clear to me that I have always been passive before being active, an effect before being a cause.

32   —One must then first be situated within sensuous circumstance in order to create signs to express first ideas acquired by sensation; and when, reflecting on this circumstance, one acquires new ideas, one creates new names whose meaning one fixes by placing others in this circumstance and by making them produce the same reflections. Then expressions would always follow ideas closely: they would therefore be clear and precise, since they would only translate what any person might have sensuously experienced.

40   —it teaches something, and thus it helps open and reveal a field of reality other than ordinary language
      —This tendency toward development distinguishes metaphor from other tropes, which are drained in their immediate expression.

41   —Sight is the sense par excellence of the imagination.

47   —His particular ideas, his comparisons, metaphors, expressions, images, constantly leading us back to nature, which we never tire of admiring, will be so many partial truths to help keep him on course.
      —Every abstraction is only a sign emptied of ideas. All abstract knowledge is only a combination of signs. Ideas have been banished by the separation of signs and things, and it is only by rejoining signs to physical objects that science can again become a science of ideas.

48   —he who supposes a new phenomenon or revives a past moment *re-creates a new world*

59   —I would have trouble saying *where* the table I am looking at is located . . . I do not situate it in its place. My gaze wanders within it as within the aura of Being; I do not see it so much as I see with it and as it invites me to see.

61   —when style is good, there is no lazy word, and when a word is not lazy, it represents a thing

68   —neighboring, sensitive instruments receive impressions which are those of the resounding instrument but not those of the thing that has transpired

70 —any writer who can, as he does, *unify* the heart by means of tenderness and *generosity* is always bound to please

71 —If this language were assumed and fixed, notions would immediately become permanent; distances would disappear; places would coalesce; bonds would be drawn between all inhabited places of the earth and all times, and all living and thinking beings would converse.

88 —Enclosing itself in language, poetry became a *distanced* description of the world.

96 —"Spoken music or remarks on subjectivity in fiction, apropos of 'Rameau's Nephew'"
—a pluralized subject . . . the semiotic trial of itself . . . the setting on trial . . . drives

99 —People used to hide certain misdeeds and would blush if they were found out. Nowadays, it seems to me, they are openly published and must, because of it, multiply, since constraint and shame used to restrain people . . . A clever man can still discover the secret of how not to be dishonored by a blamable act, if he has the courage to be the first to announce it and to tease those who might be tempted to upbraid him. People do not dare reproach him for it, seeing him take pride in it. His audacity is his justification, and reproaching him would make one seem ridiculous . . . in manners, to forestall a reproach is to destroy it . . . A man who has deceived another . . . far from feeling shame or remorse, congratulates himself on his skill . . . he simply reckons that he has won a good game of chess.

100 —the continuity of a peaceful sleep . . . plenitude of life